Walt Disney's
AMERICA

WALT DISNEY'S
AMERICA

BY CHRISTOPHER FINCH

ABBEVILLE PRESS, INC., PUBLISHERS • NEW YORK, N. Y.

For Dhimitri, for Barnaby and Hillary, for Leo,
for Alexandra and David, for Ian, for Kat and
Silver, for Sam, for Charlotte and Thomas, for
Mia, and for Chloe.

Library of Congress Cataloging in Publication Data

Finch, Christopher.
    Walt Disney's America

    1. Disney, Walt, 1901-1966. 2. Moving-picture producers and directors—
United States—Biography. 3. Animators—United States—Biography.
I. Title.
PZ1998.A3D522   791'.092'4   [B]   78-16863
ISBN 0-89659-000-3

Contents

Walt Disney's
AMERICA
A
PICTURE PREVIEW

ABOVE: *Mickey's Birthday Party,* 1942

PRECEDING PAGES: Mickey leads the Main Street parade.

ABOVE: *The Flying Squirrel,* 1954.

FOLLOWING PAGES: *Lady and the Tramp,* 1955, and
Disneyland from Town Square.

ABOVE: The riverboat *Mark Twain* at Disneyland.

OPPOSITE: Fess Parker in *Davy Crockett and the River Pirates,* 1956.

FOLLOWING PAGES: The Main Street parade at Walt Disney World, and the Walt Disney World monorail.

Introduction

A FEW YEARS AGO, I had the opportunity to write a history of the Walt Disney Studio which appeared under the title *The Art of Walt Disney*. In that book I attempted to catalogue the highlights of a remarkable career and place them in their proper setting. I tried to tell the reader a little about the development of animation from its modest beginnings to the technical splendors of *Pinocchio* and *Fantasia,* and I did my best to ascribe credit, where it was due, to the most important of Disney's associates.

Many gifted men and women have contributed to the success of the Disney enterprises but there can be no doubt that Walt Disney himself was a totally dominant figure. He ruled his studio just as Louis B. Mayer ruled at MGM and Harry Cohn reigned over Columbia Pictures but, in addition to being (in his own quiet way) a Hollywood mogul, he was also the creative head of his organization. *Snow White and the Seven Dwarfs* and Disneyland were conceived in his head. He was, so to speak, L.B. Mayer and Irving Thalberg rolled into one. In the history of the American film, only Charles Chaplin can claim to have handled both administrative and creative responsibilities so successfully.

When I was researching *The Art of Walt Disney,* Disney had been dead a little over five years, but many of the old-timers—men who had worked with him since the heyday of Mickey Mouse and the Silly Symphonies—were still active at the studio and they talked of "Walt" as if he were still alive. It was impossible to escape the feeling, which has been remarked by other visitors, that "Walt" was still peering over the shoulders of these veterans as they gathered for story conferences or worked at their animation tables. The sense of his continued presence was so strong that I half expected to arrive at the studio one day and encounter him in the corridors of the Animation Building, or lunching at his favorite table in the commissary.

Everyone is familiar with the Walt Disney who came into our homes each week, in the fifties and sixties, to introduce his enormously popular television show. This was "Uncle Walt"—an affable, mustachioed gent in a dark business suit—a friendly giant of the entertainment establishment. As I talked with old-timers about the excitement of the early days, however, I became acquainted with another Walt Disney, a younger man who seldom wore a suit or necktie, favoring jazzy Fair Isle sweaters and casual sports jackets. This preestablishment Disney gradually became as real for me as the more sober figure I knew from the television screen. This was the man who first thought of Mickey and endowed him with his own voice (raised to the pitch of a rodent countertenor). This was the man who oversaw the adventures of the Three Little Pigs and who imagined Snow White's flight through the forest of grasping trees. Photos in the Disney archive showed him to have been good-looking, in a slightly comical way—his mustache and ears giving him a faint air of being Clark Gable's smarter younger brother. The veterans told me how one of Walt's eyebrows would, in moments of stress or excitement, shoot up, independent of its more static twin, and—sure enough—there it was, captured by the camera and fixed on a forgotten contact sheet as he acted out a scene for the benefit of his artists.

It may just be the charm of the period photographs, but the young Disney—prior to World War II—seems to have had a great sense of style (and we feel this too when we watch his alter ego, Mickey, as he impersonates Fred Astaire or Ted Lewis). The later Disney—the public figure of the fifties and sixties—appears to have had little interest in style, at least with regard to his own appearance. He had one of the most familiar faces in the world, yet, and perhaps because of that fact, in dress and manner he seemed to court anonymity. This was no burned-out man—he was still capable of planning his extraordinary theme parks and of conceiving an infinitely renewable city that was intended to carry the Disney banner into the future—but it was not easy, if you were growing up in the era of television, to see the amiable figure in the dark suit as the perpetrator of some of the most inspired

Poster for *The Mad Dog*, a 1932 Mickey Mouse cartoon.

lunacies in the history of the movies, or as the author of some of the most unabashedly romantic visions ever to reach the screen. The public image did not match my idea of the kind of man who was likely to send ostriches and hippos pirouetting to "Dance of the Hours."

The young Disney, who came to life for me in recollections, letters, photographs, and snatches of old film, was another matter entirely. In those early years—as he conjured Mickey, Donald, and Goofy into being, as he stretched the art of animation to meet the challenge of the feature-length film—the creative spark was always near the surface. Photographs of the period show this quite clearly. Whether he is

At a story conference, c. 1940, Walt Disney acts out a piece of "business" for the benefit of his animation staff. Characteristically, as he becomes excited by the idea, his right eyebrow pops up.

posing with celebrities like the Barrymores, or at work with his artists, he gives off the aura of being the captain of the team—player-manager might be a more appropriate way of putting it—eager to get on with the job of his latest and most audacious game plan. And, in those early years, he was going from triumph to triumph; setbacks were rare.

It's common knowledge that Walt Disney was not a particularly gifted animator, and this had led some to suppose that his role was chiefly that of an administrator, that other people did all the real creative work. Nothing could be further from the truth. Many talented draftsmen, writers, and technicians were necessary to the realization of his projects, but Disney had an essential gift that none of the others possessed to the same extent. He was a great storyteller. This was something he was born with, but the important thing is that he taught himself how to translate this natural ability into the language of film. Through experience and application, he learned how to manipulate striking images and how to strip a plot of every excess frame of exposition.

His methods were quite straightforward. It is evident from the thousands of pages of story-conference transcripts taken by a stenographer during the production of *Snow White* that Walt Disney controlled every detail of that movie by the simple means of telling the story, over and over again, to his artists. This is not to say that he did not accept and, in fact, actively solicit ideas and creative input of all kinds from his associates—he welcomed all suggestions and used many—but only he held the whole picture in his mind, and he refined it by verbal repetition. It was up to his artists to turn his thoughts into the images that would appear on screen, but Walt described everything—characters, situations, landscapes, interiors—in such pictorial detail that each frame of the movie can legitimately be said to possess the Disney touch. Every aspect of the production received his closest attention. He did not claim to be a musician, yet he managed to retain tight control over the score and especially over the integration of the songs with the story. When it came to selecting voice talents for the various animated characters, he was scrupulous in his choices. In picking a voice for the young heroine, he had a speaker system rigged up in his office wired to the music stage, so that he could audition singers without being influenced by their appearance.

To understand Walt Disney at all, we must recognize that, during the first dozen years of his success, he was the leader of a relatively small team involved in creative decisions on a day-to-day basis. He was a man who knew how to build a stand for an animation camera, who had proved himself capable of helping to devise the first system of synchronizing sound to cartoon images, who knew how to squeeze the last laugh from the simplest gag, and who breathed life into dozens of characters, yet was prepared to help out in the ink-and-paint shop if a deadline was getting dangerously near. Later, as the head of a huge corporation, he was inevitably forced to delegate more responsibility to others—though he still stayed abreast of what was going on and contributed more than his fair share of ideas to most projects—but, to understand Disney, we must grasp the notion of the young man who could turn his hand to anything, who was prepared to work fourteen hours a day, who was never satisfied, who would roam the studio at night to familiarize himself with everything that was happening, and who was blessed with a genius for storytelling.

All these things were touched upon in *The Art of Walt Disney*, but they were not fully developed because I was concerned there with the basic task of establishing a sequence of events and giving an overview of the Disney organization as it developed during the first fifty years.

Traveling about the country to promote the book, however, I found myself talking about Walt Disney and his imagination. Interviewers were fascinated by the man and were intrigued to know what motivated him, what formed his singular sense of fantasy, what made him unique. Most were admirers of his work—a few were hostile or unconvinced—but all of them seemed to share the problem I had

31

faced of reconciling the man in the business suit with the fairy-tale world of *Snow White* and the inspired mayhem of the best of the Disney short cartoons. I tried to answer their questions as best I could and began to see the possibility of writing a different kind of book about Disney, one that would look beyond dates and events and attempt to deal with some of the more intangible elements in the Disney story.

The aspect of Disney that has most interested me is best summed up in the observation that his imagination was clearly rooted in specifically American values and was demonstrably formed by his own background, yet its appeal is universal. There is no contradiction here—blue jeans are very American but are coveted all over the world—still the implications are fascinating. Walt Disney is a universal symbol for American culture. If we understand him, we understand something about how America views the world and the world views America. Understanding Walt Disney is no simple matter, however; this is axiomatic in the fact that he is such a potent symbol. It is all too easy to see him as representing one aspect of American culture—American conservatism, for example—but such a viewpoint unjustly denies the complexities of the world that formed him.

Disney's work, it seems to me, does not reflect just one facet of the American dream. His imagination was too mercurial and protean to allow this. He was too much of a fantasist. His work, though, was shaped by fundamentally American attitudes and values. These values were so basic to his character that they informed everything he did, no matter how exotic his invention became. He was, for example, able to give definitive American form to material drawn from European folklore precisely because of this.

This book, then, is an attempt to explore some of the ways in which Walter Elias Disney was formed by America and, in his work, transformed American customs and character into the stuff of universal fantasy.

PART ONE
Main Street:

Chapter One
AMERICAN CREDENTIALS

Walt Disney with his mother, Flora, and his
sister, Ruth. Marceline, Missouri, c. 1909.

THE ESSENTIAL FACTS OF WALT DISNEY'S LIFE can be stated quite briefly. He was
born in Chicago on December 5, 1901, but spent most of his early life in
Missouri, first on a farm near the small town of Marceline, then in Kansas City.
His mother, Flora, was a former school teacher and his father, Elias—who pursued several careers—was a stern disciplinarian who preached the virtues of hard
work and disapproved of anything that smacked of entertainment or show business. In Kansas City, Walt, the fourth of five children, worked as a newspaper
boy but also sneaked out at night to take part in amateur talent contests. Elias
did permit Walt to attend drawing classes, apparently allowing that these might
be "educational." In 1917, after a brief return to Chicago—and despite the fact

that he was under age—Walt signed up as a Red Cross ambulance driver and, following the Armistice, spent several months in France before returning, in 1919, to Kansas City, where he found work in a commercial art studio. There he met a talented young draftsman named Ub Iwerks, and the two soon left to set up their own business, renting office space from a publication called *Restaurant News* before moving on to join the staff of the Kansas City Film Ad Company, which produced crude animated advertising films that were shown in local theaters.

It did not take Walt long to become convinced that he could do better work on his own. With a borrowed camera, he made a little reel of topical gags—which he called Laugh-o-Grams—for the Newman Theater, a Kansas City movie house. These were apparently well received and, though still in his teens, Disney launched the Laugh-o-Gram Company where, with the assistance of Iwerks and other young artists, he produced a series of animated fairy tales, which were updated versions of such classic fare as *Puss in Boots* and *Jack and the Beanstalk*. To make ends meet, they also worked on a variety of other projects—including a film on dental hygiene which combined animation and live-action film in a way that anticipated *Mary Poppins*—but the company did not succeed in staying afloat and, in 1923, a few months after his twenty-first birthday, Walt moved to California where his older brother, Roy, was recuperating from tuberculosis in a veterans' hospital.

Before leaving Kansas City, Walt had produced a short film titled *Alice's Wonderland* in which a live girl found herself in the company of a motley group of cartoon characters. Failing to find work with an established Hollywood studio, Walt screened *Alice's Wonderland* for a New York distributor and obtained a contract for a series of Alice comedies. Ub Iwerks and several other Kansas City colleagues joined Walt and Roy in Hollywood and, when the Alice series had run its course, they developed an all-cartoon series built around the character of Oswald the Lucky Rabbit. Oswald was successful enough to precipitate a major crisis, one which was to have a far-reaching effect on Disney's career.

A magazine cover designed by Walt Disney, in 1919, for the Newman Theater in Kansas City. This dates from the period during which Disney and Ub Iwerks operated a small commercial art studio out of the offices of a magazine called *Restaurant News.*

Ub Iwerks, Walt Disney, and Fred Harman, Kansas City, c. 1921. Disney had, by this time, formed the Laugh-o-Gram Company and was producing short cartoons based on fairy tales such as *Puss in Boots, Jack and the Beanstalk* and *Cinderella.*

Walt Disney soon after his arrival
in California, 1923.

OPPOSITE: On the set of an Alice Comedy
(l. to r.) Rudolph Ising, Roy Disney,
Red Lyon, Margie Gaye, and Walt Disney,
c. 1925.

When Walt Disney went to New York, in 1927, to renegotiate his contract with
Charles Mintz, his distributor, he was horrified to discover that Mintz in fact
owned all rights to the Oswald character and, through his brother-in-law, had
secretly engaged a number of Disney artists to take over the series. (They were
prepared to work for less money. Mintz was the first of several impresarios to
make the mistake of assuming that Disney's success derived from the talent of
his hired hands.)

According to legend—and in this case legend and truth may be one and the
same—it was on his way back to Los Angeles, aboard the Chief, that Disney came
up with a character called Mickey Mouse. (His first instinct was to call him Mor-
timer Mouse, but his wife, Lillian, persuaded him that Mickey was a snappier
name.) Back on the coast, Ub Iwerks set to work at his drawing board and provided
Mickey with his physical attributes, based on a configuration of circles that made
him instantly recognizable and, importantly, easy to animate. Walt then set about
providing the Mouse with situations that would define his character. In the wake of
the success of *The Jazz Singer*—the first significant "talkie"—Disney made the crucial decision to equip the Mouse cartoons with sound tracks, and he and his team
displayed an extraordinary ingenuity in wedding sound effects and music to Mickey's animated antics. Disney could justly claim to be one of the first masters of the
talking picture, though speech itself played a relatively small part in these early
sound cartoons, and this contributed greatly to the impact of Mickey Mouse who,
within a year or two, had become a household name.

The rest of the story is familiar. Mickey was joined by Pluto, Goofy, and Donald, along with a host of secondary characters. The Silly Symphonies, launched in 1929, allowed Disney to develop a strain of fantasy which led, in 1937, to *Snow White and the Seven Dwarfs*, his first animated feature. This was followed, during the next five years, by *Pinocchio*, *Fantasia*, *Dumbo* and *Bambi*. The wartime economy and its aftermath slowed Disney's progress but, by the early fifties, he had regained momentum and the studio began to turn out new animated features and live-action films, and soon it branched out into television. The big leap of the fifties, however, was Disneyland—built against all informed advice—and this came to absorb more and more of Walt Disney's energies. By the time he died, in 1966, construction of a far more extensive resort area and theme park, Walt Disney World, was already under way—its essential character masterminded by Walt himself.

What we have here is, on the surface, a classic American success story. The United States does not own a patent on the self-made man but there can be little doubt that, in the past century and a half, the species has thrived here as nowhere else. Had Horatio Alger lived a couple of generations later, he might have dreamed up a hero like Walt Disney.

But we should not make the mistake of seeing Walt Disney as being entirely typical of the genre. He did become a captain of industry—the man in the business suit again—but he did not get there by inventing a better mouse trap, then sitting back and raking in the royalties. He did not achieve success by building a chain of motels, each cloned from the last, or by franchising a cheaper way of mass-produc-

TOP: A scene from *Steamboat Willie*, 1928,
the first sound cartoon. Center and bottom:
Scenes from *Plane Crazy*, 1928.

ing hamburgers. He was, first and foremost, a great popular artist, and his unflagging need to invent new forms of entertainment drove him to take constant risks that would have been unthinkable in a more conventional business enterprise. (Until the last few years of his life, he was not a very wealthy man since he constantly ploughed back company profits and his own capital into new and often highly speculative projects.) The organization he built is now an extremely diversified one, but this came about not just because of the ordinary corporate desire to broaden the company's fiscal base but because every so often he felt an urge to reinvent some branch or other of the entertainment industry.

There is a strain of American idealism which likes to believe that art and business are, or should be, separate entities. The act of writing a book or making a painting may have nothing to do with business, but anyone who has signed a contract with a publisher or exhibited a painting in a gallery can tell you that the two worlds inevitably overlap. We tend to admire the nineteenth-century concept of the bohemian artist—Van Gogh half-mad and poverty-stricken—but this should not blind us to the fact that most major artists have not, in fact, courted hunger or chosen to live in a garret. Throughout history, poets and painters have sought patronage, often becoming skillful businessmen in the process. The masters of the Renaissance turned to popes and merchant princes; the Hollywood film maker has had to turn to the American public.

Walt Disney's success was always predicated on the fact that he was uncannily in tune with the American public. In a very real sense, American popular taste is the subject and essence of his work. Those who deplore American popular taste—and we would be blind if we could not see its lapses—are likely to be unsympathetic to Disney. Those who appreciate its energy and vigor, on the other hand, and who are prepared to take the good with the bad, will find much to admire and enjoy in the Disney product.

Interestingly, foreign critics, who perceive American popular culture as an homogeneous whole, tend to have less difficulty with it than do many home-grown

pundits who seem confused by day-to-day shifts in taste. Europeans and South Americans may be legitimately disturbed by the Americanization of their own culture but it would be absurd to suggest that American popular culture is inappropriate to the United States. The fact that Disney is so blatantly American makes his work fascinating for domestic and overseas audiences alike.

As an exponent of a popular art form that could come to fruition only through the patronage of a massive public and the labor of hundreds of employees, Disney inevitably had to face the realities of the business world, but those realities never dominated his thinking. He was an entertainer by vocation, a businessman by necessity. According to his co-workers, he was never very happy dealing with the daily affairs of a big corporation, preferring to leave such matters to his brother Roy and other officers of the company, but inevitably he did make the major decisions, which was only appropriate since his imagination was the company's chief commodity.

There are critics who argue that the products of Disney's imagination do not constitute "art" at all, and Walt Disney himself concurred in this opinion. "I've never called my work an 'art,' " he once remarked. "It's part of show business, the business of building entertainment." Such a comment may have been intended chiefly to disarm criticism—the last thing he wanted was aestheticians telling him that he was falling short of the standards set by Tolstoi—but he was also pointing out that our enjoyment of Mickey Mouse or Disneyland does not depend on any definition of art. (Though let us concede, at least, that Disney's best work displays great artistry.) The fact is that Walt Disney did not set out to be an artist in the sense that Cézanne and Picasso were artists. His initial ambition was to take the language of the animated cartoon, a humble medium by any standards, and enrich it to the point where it could carry a fairly elaborate story of sufficient general interest to entertain a huge audience consisting of both adults and children.

It was only natural that he should turn to the established conventions of Hollywood and popular literature—melodrama and folksy comedy, with their attendant values of sentimentality and "cuteness"—to provide him with a framework. With very few exceptions, the early masters of the American cinema, including such eminences as Chaplin and D.W. Griffith, all indulged in sentimental excesses. Like them, Disney was forging a new language—animation was fifteen or twenty years behind the live-action film in technical sophistication at the close of the silent era—and we must forgive his occasional lapses of taste that would be startling in, say, the work of a major novelist of the same period. The novelist was working within an established tradition and could concentrate on refinements of sentiment, language, and idiom. Disney, by contrast, was creating a new form. It was as if he was forced to re-invent the internal combustion engine while they could afford to customize Rolls Royces and Dusenbergs. We should judge Disney's early work—up to 1942, let us say—by the incredible vigor, skill, and invention that he brought to creating a viable language for the animated film.

The early history of the cinema is characterized by the discovery of new ways to tell old stories. The silent comedians, it's true, and Disney too in his short cartoons, used the technical possibilities of the camera—slow motion, for example—to create effects that could be achieved in no other medium; beyond that, however, their story conventions were ancient. This, indeed, is a partial explanation of the success of the movies. Film makers, unencumbered by tradition, could make the old seem new.

When we are viewing Hollywood movies of the "Golden Age," what fascinates us is not so much the stories themselves but the way in which they are told. That is where the artistry lies. The best Hollywood pictures have a kind of divine simplicity and obviousness that makes them immensely satisfying. The happy ending does not encourage great psychological subtlety, but it does—as has always been the case with fairy tales—provide a wonderful abstract framework for the skillful storyteller to work with. Hollywood could not compete with Shakespeare, but it did find a modern equivalent for the morality play, and that was no mean achievement.

The live-action films produced by the great Hollywood studios had the advantage

TOP: **The Main Street of Marceline, Missouri, c. 1906, and,** BOTTOM: Main Street in Disneyland.

of larger-than-life personalities—Mary Pickford, Clark Gable, Greta Garbo—to give them substance and to bring human warmth to the abstractions of the screenplays. What makes Disney's achievement so remarkable is that he and his artists were forced to invent their stars from scratch. These headliners were born in story conferences and on sketch pads, yet Mickey and Donald and the rest became as celebrated throughout the land as any live stars who performed on the sound stages at MGM or Warner Brothers.

It cannot be denied that Disney—especially later in his career—produced movies in which the weaknesses of the Hollywood formulae swamped the strengths, but I believe that, like any other artist, he deserves to be judged by his best work, and there is a considerable body of that. The classic short cartoons of the thirties and forties, and the first half-dozen animated features are masterpieces—some flawed, some almost perfect—and no one who is not thoroughly familiar with them can presume to make a judgment on Walt Disney's artistry.

There remain two masterpieces of a different kind—Disneyland and Walt Disney World—and these bring us face-to-face again with Disney's essentially American character. (The symbolism is quite clear. In both theme parks, an exquisite reproduction of an American small town Main Street leads to Disney's romanticized versions of the past and the future.)

In my earlier book, I described these parks as being a twentieth-century equivalent of Versailles—a remark that caused some raising of eyebrows—and I still hold to this. I do not mean to suggest that they contain architectural marvels to match the Palace of Versailles, the Trianons, or the Orangery, but as pleasure gardens there are many parallels to be found. The difference is that whereas André Le Nôtre planned the grounds of Versailles for the enjoyment of French aristocrats, Walt Disney planned his parks for the enjoyment of the American family. French courtiers won the privilege of enjoying the ground of Versailles by right of birth and inherited wealth. Disney's theme parks are open to anyone who can afford the relatively modest admission fee. This dictates a substantial difference in taste but does not destroy the parallel. In the time of Louis XIV, the Grand Canal at Versailles was covered with Venetian gondolas. The great lagoons in the Disney parks are home to paddle-wheelers and rafts from the world of Mark Twain. The statuary that decorates the yew-lined alleys of Versailles evokes the Arcadian phase of classical literature. The audio-animatronic figures that are so much a part of the Disney parks' entertainment conjure up memories of the adventure yarns of everyone's childhood. More ponderous statues at Versailles celebrate great political figures such as Richelieu, Condé, and the Sun King himself. At Walt Disney World, the Hall of Presidents contains the likenesses of great American leaders. Versailles and the Disney parks are separated by a vast cultural chasm, but each in its own way celebrates similar pleasures and pieties. Each reflects the culture that produced it, while all three remain essentially fantasies, removed from the everyday realities of life.

More parallels can be found. Each of these parks uses water to great effect—evidently it served the same magical purpose now as then—and at both Versailles and Walt Disney World enormous engineering projects were needed to bring this about. Fundamentally, though, the point is that the Disney parks are the great pleasure grounds of the latter half of the twentieth century and, like Versailles, they are archetypal expressions of the taste of their time.

In the theme parks, the Main Street areas are virtually a statement of Walt Disney's cultural credo. As a child he had known hard times. The family never had much money and, before he was in his teens, young Walt knew what it was to set off for work at 3:30 on a frigid morning, and he evidently grew up with an enduring passion for the street life of Middle America.

As a small boy, in the years that his parents operated the farm in Linn County, Missouri, we can be sure that he often visited the nearby town of Marceline. Such early experiences have a way of staying with a man and of taking on a mellow glow with the passage of time. It's not difficult to imagine that Marceline's main thoroughfare must have seemed a fascinating place to an impressionable young mind. During those formative years, this was the Athens and Rome of Walt Disney's world. The activities that he glimpsed through the windows and open doorways of the barber shop, the haberdashery, and the general store fed his imagination. It would have been to this environment that he attached his early memories of Christmas, perhaps of his first Fourth of July parade. It may have been on the Main Street of Marceline that he saw his first automobile. His later love of railroads can be traced to the fact that the tracks of the Atchison, Topeka, and Santa Fe ran through Marceline en route for Kansas City and California.

The Kansas City experience gave him a chance to expand his vision of America, and this would have been heightened by his brief return to Chicago. His service in France widened his horizons even further and he arrived in Los Angeles, still a young man, in time to witness its extraordinary growth from a provincial town into a major metropolis; but Marceline must have been at the core of his memories and of his concept of America. The Main Streets he constructed in his parks are not exact reproductions of Marceline or any other small town—they are too well paved, too well maintained, and there is too much gilt in the lettering on the store fronts— but the memory is there. Disney was far too smart to believe that the American public wanted an exact reconstruction. He thought in archetypes and so he conceived an idealized version of the past in which everything is as it should have been. He understood very well that nostalgia tends to blur images. What he did was to take those misty images and give them a renewed sharpness of detail that was well researched and faithful to its sources, but which eliminated imperfections and evidence of decay.

Decay is always apparent in the real world. If we are talking of streets and architecture, in the normal course of things brickwork becomes eroded by wind and rain, boards rot, paint peels from window frames. Even a well-maintained building displays inevitable signs of use, however slight. Disney was as aware of this as anyone. For his Main Streets he wanted to rescue a moment in time—or, more accurately, a synthesis of moments—from the continuum of history. Everything about this archi-

Looking down on Disneyland's Main Street.

tecture is calculated to sustain that effect. Even the scale has been subtly altered to make it seem more intimate. In a sense, this robs it of reality—and the reality of, say, Marceline in 1909 is, in any case, lost forever—but the crowds who throng Disney's Main Streets on a busy summer day bring their own reality with them. They wear blue jeans and T-shirts or Hawaiian shirts, cameras dangle from their necks— they are light years removed from their great-grandparents who inhabited the models on which this architecture is based—but they connect with the past and they restore it to the world of the living and concrete present.

The symbolic values of Main Street are at the center of the Disney aesthetic. He had an imagination which could stretch itself to cover much of the world and many periods of history, but Marceline, circa 1909, always remained home base.

Chapter Two
DISNEYLAND

Walt Disney talks to one of the
street entertainers in Disneyland.

IT IS WORTH TAKING A DETAILED LOOK at the genesis and planning of Disneyland because its completion was one of the milestones of Walt Disney's career, and the story tells us much about the way the man thought and worked. In particular, we can see how his major ideas tended to grow out of his own life experience and his response to his native environment.

Amusement parks were not a novelty in southern California. For many years, the piers at Venice, Ocean Park, and Santa Monica were the sites of large amusement areas of the Coney Island type, complete with side shows, fun houses, giant roller coasters, and all the traditional midway attractions. In the silent era, these often provided a background for Hollywood movies. By the late forties, however, most of these operations had fallen on hard times or had been closed down entirely. The public was demanding something more sophisticated, and most entrepreneurs interpreted this as meaning that all amusement parks were doomed to eventual extinction. Disney thought otherwise. His interpretation of the phenomenon was that people wanted a different kind of amusement park, but he found few professionals who would agree with him. When he was researching the feasibility of Disneyland, he sent aides all over the country, seeking the advice of acknowledged experts in the field. The advice these experts handed out was unanimous: "Forget about building an amusement park. It's certain to be a disaster." Disney recalled that other experts had predicted that *Snow White* would be a failure and pressed ahead with his scheme.

Disney had been thinking about his park for a very long time. When his daughters were youngsters, he often took them to a little amusement area on La Cienega Boulevard where they had a good time but he found himself becoming bored. "I'd sit," he once explained, "while they rode the merry-go-round and did all those things—sit on a bench, you know, eating peanuts. I felt there should be something built where the parents and the children could have fun together. So that's how Disneyland started . . . it was a period of maybe fifteen years developing."

During this period of gestation, he modified his plans many times. At first he seems to have thought of a modest playground at the studio itself, one that would feature rides built around Disney characters. Nothing came of this, though it was a project he was fond of talking about. Impetus for a rather grander kind of park came in part from a hobby that Disney took up right after the war.

Walt had always been fascinated by railroads. Trains were one of his boyhood obsessions and, when his doctor suggested that he was working too hard and needed a hobby, he turned back to that world. (Until shortly before the war, he had played polo for relaxation, but his backers eventually insisted that he give up the sport, fearing that he might be seriously injured.) Two of Disney's top animators, Ward Kimball and Ollie Johnston, were already serious railroad

TOP: The Santa Fe depot in Marceline, Missouri, c. 1906. CENTER: Walt Disney at work on one of his scale model locomotives. BOTTOM: Walt Disney with a model of Disneyland's New Orleans Square.

AT RIGHT AND OPPOSITE: **Making friends in Disneyland.**
PRECEDING PAGES: The Disneyland locomotive;
Ernest A. Marsh, takes on water.

buffs, and Walt picked up many tips from them, then began to construct his
own backyard railroad, building much of the rolling stock with his own hands.

In the early years of the studio, Disney had had plenty of opportunities to use
his hands—some department always needed help to meet a deadline—but gradually
these evaporated as he found himself more and more involved with the conceptual
side of film making. Building his miniature railroad restored to him a valued activity; but inevitably, given his imagination, it also evoked a whole new range of
possibilities. He must have remembered the roar of the big Santa Fe locomotives as
they rushed through Marceline, the excitement of the small-town depot. Before
long, he was talking about running a railroad around the Burbank studio, and soon
this impulse became attached to his notion of a new kind of amusement park.
Transportation and nostalgia, he saw, could be a big factor in making his park
different.

Between the Disney lot and the Los Angeles River was a tract of undeveloped
land which today carries a stretch of the Ventura Freeway, and Walt thought
about acquiring this for his scheme, but he decided it was not large enough. Once
committed to an idea, he was incapable of not developing it to its logical conclusion, and the concept of Disneyland began to expand in his mind and on paper until
it became evident that a site of two or three hundred acres would be required.

At this point, Disney commissioned the Stanford Research Institute to scout
locations for him. The institute's recommendation was that he purchase a large
tract of orange groves in Anaheim, south of Los Angeles, close to the proposed

route of the Santa Ana Freeway which was then under construction. At that
time, Anaheim was relatively isolated, but the freeway would bring it within a
short drive of the major Los Angeles residential neighborhoods, while Orange
County, where Anaheim is situated, was rapidly becoming urbanized too.

The site was perfect for Disney's purposes, and his plans for the park began
to take definitive shape. (Eventually, a new corporation, WED—for Walter Elias
Disney—was set up to supervise the planning.) There remained the matter of
financing the park and this, given the experts' doubts about its feasibility, was not
an easy matter.

Disney put much of his own money into the early planning of Disneyland, even
selling his weekend home in Palm Springs to raise cash, but major backers were
needed, and eventually two companies came forward with the funding. One was
Western Printing and Lithography, a publishing company that had had a long
association with the Disney organization. The other was the American Broadcasting Company.

In the early fifties, ABC was running a distant third to NBC and CBS in the
rapidly developing television market. All three networks had approached Disney
with a view to having him originate a series for them. He had agreed to produce
a couple of specials but had fought shy of the series idea, perhaps because he had
had bad luck with a radio series several years earlier. ABC, however, had much to
gain by persuading Disney to join its lineup and finally an agreement was
reached. Disney would produce the Disneyland series for ABC and, in return,

FOLLOWING PAGES: Disneyland's Town Square.

Vintage vehicles meet at Disneyland's Main Street.

ABC would put up a substantial amount of capital to help finance the park. Since the series would help promote the park, this seemed satisfactory all around. Disney had already persuaded thirty companies to lease concessions in the proposed park, which brought in more capital, and Walt Disney Productions was able to raise a sum equal to the ABC investment. Eventually, acting on a prior agreement, the Disney organization bought out both ABC and Western.

Disneyland opened in July of 1955, and it soon became clear that it would be a great success. From this point on, the Disney organization would have few financial worries and Walt Disney himself, finally, would become a wealthy man, though he did not change his modest life-style.

Disneyland was far more than just a financial triumph, however; it was a totally new kind of entertainment complex and it was to become a symbol of the age—the ultimate American pleasure ground, a kind of permanent Fourth of July celebration. A few quotes will serve to show exactly what Walt Disney was aiming for when he built the first of his Magic Kingdoms:

Disneyland is like Alice stepping through the looking glass.

The Disneyland monorail passes gracefully above a lagoon as
one of the park's fleet of submarines sets out on a mission.

**To step through the portals of Disneyland will be like entering
another world.**

**Disneyland would be a world of Americans, past and present,
seen through the eyes of my imagination – a place of warmth and
nostalgia, of illusion and color and delight.**

**Disneyland will be the essence of America as we know it, the
nostalgia of the past with exciting glimpses of the future. It will
give meaning to the pleasure of children – and pleasure to the
experience of adults . . . It will be a place for the people to find
happiness and knowledge.**

The layout of the park was an important factor contributing to its success, as
Disney clearly recognized:

**"The more I go to other amusement parks . . . the more I am
convinced of the wisdom of the original concept of Disneyland. I
mean, have a single entrance through which all the traffic would
flow, then a hub off which the various areas were situated. This**

61

**gives people a sense of orientation – they know where they are at
all times. And it saves a lot of walking."**

These practical considerations were important, but so was the symbolism since,
as already noted, the single entrance opened onto Town Square and Main Street,
and Main Street became the way into Adventureland, Fantasyland, Frontierland,
and Tomorrowland. The layout of Disneyland is like a diagram of Walt Disney's
imagination.

No matter how well the park was conceived, however, it would not have worked
if the plan had not been executed with a sharp sense of quality and detail. People
visiting Disneyland for the first time are often surprised by the craftmanship
which is evident on all sides. This is a world of illusion, but the props are startling-
ly real, and we must remember that the movie industry has had long experience in
conjuring up other times and other places. The Western towns and European
squares that can be found on Hollywood back lots may consist of nothing but false
fronts attached to crude frameworks, but they are remarkably convincing.
Disneyland is, in fact, like a gigantic back lot open to the public, with the important difference that its false façades conceal rides and entertainments rather than
storage space for generators and lighting equipment.

We must realize, too, that the people who planned Disneyland—from Walt Disney
down—were mostly men who had spent their life in the movie industry. Many were
graduates of the animation department. They brought to the park the same imagination that they had brought to screen entertainment. Characters and situations
developed in Disney movies also provided the basis for many of the park's rides.

Everything has been carefully considered. The scale of Main Street has been
subtly altered—the upper stories are not quite as tall as they would be in a real
town—so that a feeling of intimacy is produced (especially in contrast to the glass-
and-steel canyons of modern cities). Main Street makes visitors feel a little larger
than life. The architecture is not a pastiche of turn-of-the-century styles—it is an
immaculate reproduction. No corners have been cut. Every detail, down to the last

piece of gingerbread fretwork, is made exactly as it would have been made in 1900. The charming art of the sign painter is everywhere in evidence, and the vintage cars and horse-drawn trolleys are exactly what you might have seen in any American town in the early years of the century. (Disney made a deliberate decision to capture the brief period in which the automobile had arrived but had not yet displaced the horse-drawn vehicle.)

Walt Disney had a hard childhood and knew as well as anyone else that "the good old days" were not all good, but he also understood that they take on a new significance as they slip into the past. Memory tends to strip the past of its quotidian hardships while abstracting the positive values that transcend the shifts of circumstance. Disney made every effort to sharpen our picture of the past by focusing on those details which seem significant in retrospect. Disneyland's Main Street and the adjacent Town Square area (which Walt could survey from his private apartment above the fire station) are designed to evoke old values, a sense of neighborhood and the compactness of society in a simpler age.

Walt Disney was a conservative man in that he believed that such old values retain their usefulness, if only as a reminder of what was once viable. I think it is fair to say that, for him, Main Street was a metaphor for a way of life governed by what can only be called common sense, and his belief in the validity of common sense permeated everything he did. Of course, the paradox of Disney is that his common-sense approach was always allied with a highly developed instinct for the creation of fantasy. It is the fantasy that lends an aura of enchantment to the Magic Kingdom—what other Main Street leads to a castle from the once-upon-a-time world of the Brothers Grimm?—but the fact that it is rooted in easily understood values makes the fabulous all the more accessible to the millions of visitors who enjoy it annually.

A horse-drawn bus approaches Town Square.

Chapter Three
ONCE UPON A TIME

Walt Disney conducts a story meeting, c. 1941.

THE AMERICA THAT WALT DISNEY GREW UP IN was very different from the one we know today. The memory of the frontier was still very real, especially in towns like Marceline, and the pace of life was much slower. It seems certain that Walt Disney did not see his first movie until after the family moved to Kansas City. He was an adult before radio became a factor in the home life of Americans, and he was middle-aged when television began to be a major phenomenon. In short, his mind was formed at a time when—in small-town America, anyway—the written word still reigned supreme.

A number of Disney films begin with the familiar device of a book being opened so that the scene can be set with the help of the written word. Generally, the first thing the viewer is confronted with is a variant on some time-honored phrase such as "Long ago in a distant land," or "Once upon a time"—a relic of a still more ancient tradition, the spoken word.

By all accounts, Walt Disney in person was a spellbinding storyteller. He could bring his movies to life—for his animators or for prospective backers—before a single image had been committed to celluloid, acting out every character, filling each scene with relevant detail, and building slowly toward the appropriate climax. On social occasions, he was apt to keep guests entertained with, for example, an account of a camping trip which he transformed into a comic adventure, complete with sound effects that would encompass everything from a prowling bear to the different snores that emerged from various tents. We have all met people with this kind of gift; what made Walt Disney special was his ability to turn it into images that captivated people in darkened theaters all over the world.

There is a certain amount of luck in any success story. Disney received his fair share when he discovered his ideal medium, animation, at a very early age. He had been interested in drawing and cartooning from early childhood, but had he not taken the job with the Kansas City Film Ad Company he might never have thought of adapting his talent to the needs of the cinema. There is reason to believe, too, that the failure of his Laugh-o-Gram Company made him think twice about the future of animation. Had he found work at a major Hollywood studio, he might well have distinguished himself in some more conventional branch of film making, but he would never have had the autonomy to realize his full potential, nor the opportunity to bring animation to technical maturity. Along the Main Street of Walt Disney's America, the possession of "know-how" was a very desirable attribute. Walt was "know-how" personified, and "know-how" was the lifeblood of the embryo art of animation.

The ideal animation producer should know a little about both art and the mechanics of the motion-picture camera; he should know something of the rudiments of human anatomy and of animal locomotion; he should have some understanding of modern management methods; he should know the capabilities and potential of each of his artists, and he should have enough knowledge of each of their specialties to be capable of demonstrating exactly what he wants from

TOP: An ink-and-paint girl works on Mickey. CENTER: A view of the old Walt Disney studio on Hyperion Avenue in Los Angeles. BOTTOM: Filming a penguin for animators to study.

As this 1932 picture shows, theaters held over *The Three Little Pigs* for weeks and even months.

them; he should be an inspired tinkerer and he *must* be a master story editor. This ideal animation producer would be, in short, a combination of Norman Rockwell, Henry Ford, and Mark Twain—and Walt Disney came close to being just that.

Animated films are not like books or paintings. Their production is far removed from the romantic concept of the individual artist facing a blank canvas and turning it into a masterpiece (though the hand of the individual should still be evident in the final product). The animated film requires much purely mechanical work and even the shortest cartoon engages the skills of many people. The men and women who draw and paint the images that appear on screen cannot indulge in any gratuitous self-expression. The animation drawings and background paintings they produce are often beautiful in themselves, but they are valueless unless they contribute to the whole, and the whole is bound together by the story. If an animated film has a weak story line, all the skills of the animators go to waste.

Many storytellers have a tendency to excess; they seem to become hypnotized by their own skill and embroider endlessly. The techniques of the animated film make this impossible, or at least unfeasible. The man-hours involved in animating a single, simple scene is staggering, so that each foot of film costs far more than equivalent footage using live actors (no matter how highly paid). Live-action directors, as a matter of course, shoot far more footage than they will actually need and discard much of it in the editing room. In the animation field, such a process would be hopelessly extravagant and so the editing must be done in advance, before any

A recording session for a Mickey Mouse cartoon. Walt Disney is seated at bottom left.

footage is animated or shot. For once, economics benefits art. Whoever is responsible for the overall structure of an animated film must plan it carefully in advance and is obliged to strip his story of all gratuitous and unnecessary elements. So it was that Walt Disney learned to tell a story with brevity and effectiveness.

The importance of story sense cannot be emphasized too much since it was this that gave Disney his dominance in the field. To illustrate this, we might look at what happened to Ub Iwerks when, in the early thirties, he launched his own studio. Iwerks was the greatest animator of that period and—a near-genius when it came to technical problems and the gadgetry of film making—he certainly out-muscled Disney when it came to sheer "know-how." But he lacked story sense. He could not create situations that gave his characters life. He did not know how to organize a series of gags into a coherent whole with a beginning, a middle, and an end. Iwerks' characters, like Flip the Frog, came nowhere near rivaling Mickey and Donald, and eventually Iwerks returned to the Disney fold as the studio's resident inventor. In later years, he developed a technique for Xeroxing animation drawings on celluloid, thus saving literally millions of man-hours, and his special-effects work on *Mary Poppins* won him an Academy Award.

Because of the need to edit in advance and to give the animators a pictorial sense of the action, the "screenplay" of a cartoon is worked out on a series of storyboards. The storyboard—which first came into use at the Disney studio in the early thirties—is a kind of comic strip in which every image and its accompanying dialogue

71

are on a separate sheet of paper, all of them pinned to a large corkboard. (In the case of a feature film, as many as sixty or seventy boards may be needed.) If a scene does not work, images can be rearranged, replaced, or eliminated. The whole thing is juggled until everyone concerned is satisfied that it will play on screen. Then the storyboard is photographed and blowups are distributed to all the artists who will be working on the scene.

This system was ideally suited to Disney's own abilities. He could wander from room to room and see the work of his story artists spread out in front of him on the walls. With his ability to visualize how something would strike an audience, he could tell in a moment what needed to be changed. (He seems to have had a particular and surprisingly rare gift for spotting the *obvious* solution to a given story problem, the solution that had been *too* obvious for the average person to recognize.) Disney himself did not, of course, generate all story ideas—dozens of people contributed to the content of a Disney feature—but he knew exactly which ones would work, and why, and which ones should be thrown out, and he knew how to fit everything together. He honed his skills on the shorts of the thirties, in which a sometimes complex story had to be told in seven or eight minutes, and brought them to the peak of efficiency with *Snow White.* No one else in the animation field has matched him in the abstract organization of story elements.

It remains, of course, for talented animators to bring the characters to life on screen, but these characters already live in the story sketches. It is my opinion that the essential artistry of the animated film is exercised in the story conference. Much of what comes after is fundamentally mechanical.

This is not to say that Disney was indifferent to the mechanical aspects. He was constantly striving to improve technique in all phases of production, and there is, I think, something peculiarly American in this combination of intuitive artistry and extreme technical competence. The successes of pioneer technocrats like Thomas Edison—visionaries with "know-how"—had given Americans of Walt Disney's

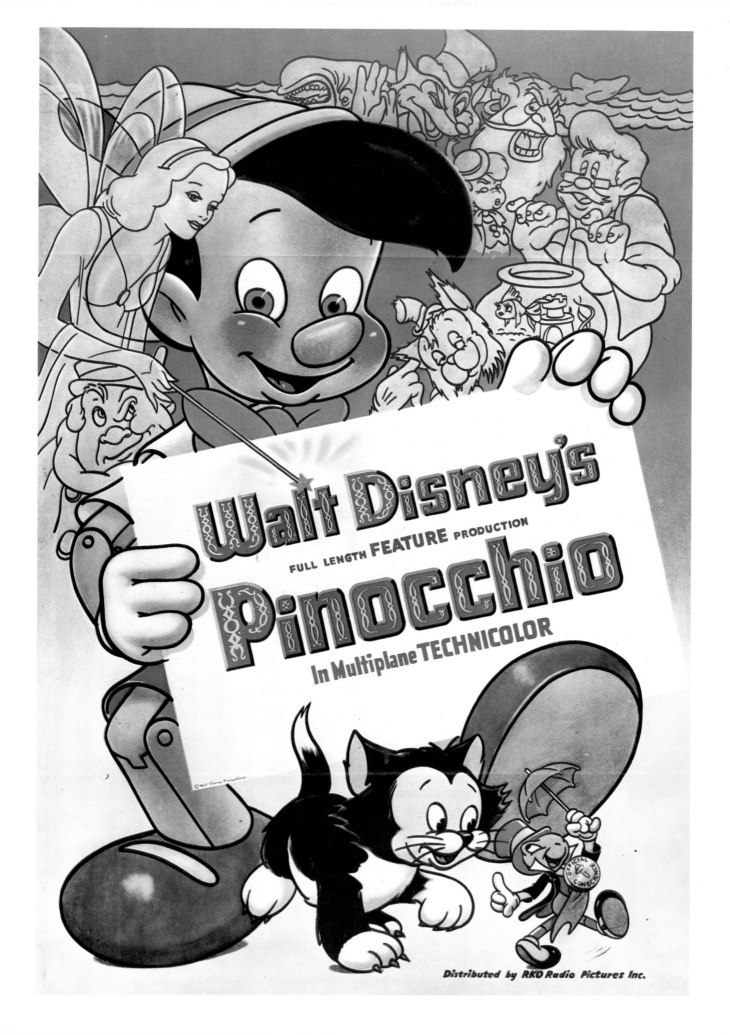

generation a great faith in a certain kind of technical achievement. For them, technology was not dull. Anyone who had peered beneath the hood of a Model A Ford, or seen one of the Wright Brothers' biplanes soar against the sky knew that technology could be magical and could transform the world. The very primitiveness of early automobiles, phonographs, radios, and telephones added to their charm and mystique. They pointed to the future but their appearance—the craftsmanship that went into them—often echoed the past.

The art of animation, in the thirties, was itself a kind of primitive technology, with new improvements arriving almost daily. The elegantly carpentered animation tables and the primitive-looking Movieolas on which the artists viewed their progress gave the animators' rooms something of the appearance of a late Victorian laboratory or workshop. Automation was impossible—the human hand had to be evident at every stage—yet many phases of animation recalled life on the production line. Picture, for example, the lot of the "in-betweener." A senior animator might be responsible for every fourth or sixth drawing in a given sequence. It was left to the "in-betweener" to fill in the intervening drawings, so that the movement would appear smooth on screen.

The Disney artists found a happy middle course that allowed them to take advantage of technology without letting it swamp them. The early cartoons possess much the same kind of charm that one finds in a vintage car. One admires the engineering beneath the hood, but one is also impressed by the old-fashioned elegance of the coachwork. Again, these are the values of Main Street.

Clearly, an ability to set up a counterpoint between two different kinds of activity and two apparently contradictory aesthetics was crucial to the later success of the Disney theme parks. The authenticity of period detail gives them much of their character, yet if Disney had not felt comfortable with the world of technology, had not, in fact, had an abiding love of gadgetry, he could not have conceived of many of the parks' attractions. The audio-animatronic robots—animated figures in three dimensions—are an astounding concept, taking advantage of up-to-date electronic circuitry and servomechanisms. Beneath Walt Disney World is an enormous computer complex controlling all the rides in the park, and even the music played in the lobbies of the nearby hotels. (If such efficiency sounds a little terrifying, it should be emphasized that it is swamped on the surface by the crowds and by the profusion of fantastic invention. The park may be run by computer but it was not conceived by computer.)

In a very real sense, the parks are intended to be "read" like a story. They are laid out so that the traffic flow—while no patterns are forced on the visitor—permits one to move naturally from scene to scene, as in a movie. The parks were, of course, designed by film makers, not city planners, and they thought naturally in terms of narrative flow. Disney wished to avoid, at all costs, the World's Fair kind of exhibit in which each pavilion is competing with every other for attention. Nor are his parks anything like the Coney Island type of amusement park which relies on noise and confusion to generate excitement. The Disney parks, for all their wealth of entertainment, are almost genteel by comparison. Except for special events, such as fireworks' displays and electrical parades, most of the thrills are experienced indoors.

A walk down Main Street, or through Frontierland, is like being told the story of America's past. "Here is a movie theater showing Fatty Arbuckle films, and there is a horse drawn trolley car. . . " And it is only appropriate that the hand of the storyteller should be evident in the parks since Disney launched them with the power of the spoken word. When he was hatching Disneyland—and anticipating that everyone would be made extremely nervous by the project—he took key people aside, one by one, and painted a word picture of this marvelous place he intended to build: a place where both adults and children could have a good time; a place that would look to the past and to the future; a place that would turn every day into the Fourth of July. Each of these people, warned to keep this project a secret, felt himself to be the custodian of privileged information. By the time Walt made his first public announcement about his plans to build Disneyland, most of his staff had been briefed in this way and had been infected with Walt's enthusiasm.

Chapter Four
MICKEY AND HIS EXTENDED FAMILY

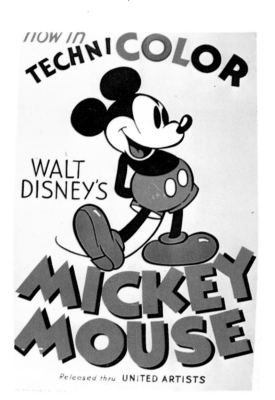

Mickey Mouse in his heyday.

WALT DISNEY'S GREATEST TRIBUTE to the America he grew up in—the world of Main Street he had to leave behind as success overtook him—is the marvelous series of short cartoons starring Mickey Mouse, Minnie, Donald Duck, Goofy, Pluto, and all their many furred and feathered friends. This saga began in the twenties and continued into the sixties. Its heyday, however, was from 1928 to the early forties. The concept of animal characters serving as human surrogates, for literary and dramatic purposes, goes back to Aesop's fables and beyond. Aesop's animals discourse like people, as do the birds of Aristophanes and the creatures that populate La Fontaine's *Fables*. The inside-out world of Lewis Carroll's imagination allowed his Alice to rub shoulders with highly verbal caterpillars and March hares, and Edward Lear's verses introduce us to a number of articulate animals. Mickey

This is a C.U. of Clarabelle Cow standing on platform playing
a base fiddle. As she sways from side to side with an exaggerated movement, the base fiddle bends back and forth to the action. Clarabelle Cow
is wearing the usual skirt which also swings back and forth as she sways.
This is a repeat of the same drawings thruout.

FOOTAGE 8-

A page from the story book prepared for an early Mickey Mouse cartoon.

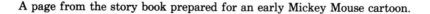

Mouse not only talks, he also drives a car, lives in a house, plays various musical instruments, listens to the radio, eats with a knife and fork, and generally behaves like a man in every important particular. He even owns a pet dog, Pluto, the only important character from the early short cartoons who is truly an animal, though even he displays human characteristics at times.

There were at least two good reasons for using animals as human surrogates in the early part of Disney's career. First, they make wonderful archetypal characters. Donald Duck, for example, is the ultimate irascible paranoid in a way that no human character—except perhaps the marvelous W.C. Fields—could possibly be. Second, and on a more practical level, animation was at a relatively primitive level when Disney started out—his artists were still acquiring their skills and refining

An early Mickey Mouse promotion, tied in with a stage show, 1931.

their vocabulary—and animals are much easier to animate than men and women. The reason for this is easy enough to understand. We all know how a man walks, or how a woman moves as she descends a staircase. The least stiffness or inaccuracy will therefore appear jarring on screen. On the other hand, whoever saw a mouse walking on two feet? Especially a mouse that appears to be about as tall as Mickey Rooney, has large circular ears, and wears bright red shorts and shoes that resemble a pair of matched bumper cars. First drawn by Ub Iwerks, Mickey was later modified and streamlined by Freddy Moore and other Disney artists, but he always remained a character who allowed the animators to improvise freely without having to be too concerned about falling into anatomical errors.

TOP: *Lonesome Ghosts,* 1937. CENTER: *Lend a Paw,* 1941. BOTTOM: *The Worm Turns,* 1937.

OPPOSITE: **Scenes from** *Mickey's Polo Team,* 1936, **and** *Mickey's Garden,* 1935.

ABOVE: Although he seldom drew in earnest after about 1928, here Walt Disney poses at a drawing board.

AT RIGHT: Animators at work in the old Hyperion Avenue studio.

Young animators, training at the Disney studio in the thirties, were taught that Mickey Mouse was a typical small-town American—sometimes a young adult, sometimes just a boy—and the extended family of creatures that grew up around him belonged to the same environment, though they were not averse to excursions to the big city and occasionally found themselves in even more exotic climes. Even if their adventures took them to the land of the Arabian Nights, however, their values remained those of Marceline and a thousand other modest communities. Mickey's adventures abroad were like the dream life of a newsboy inspired by the

ABOVE: Mickey meets another big star of the early thirties, MGM's Jackie Cooper.

AT RIGHT: Mickey Mouse watches, some selling for as little as a dollar, were enormously popular in the thirties, as can be judged from this store display.

adventures of Rudolph Valentino and Douglas Fairbanks. In his waking life, he was more at home on a street car or at a county fair.

Minnie was with him from the very beginning, appearing in *Plane Crazy,* the first Mouse cartoon to be animated, and in *Steamboat Willie,* the first to be released. Pegleg Pete also made his debut in *Steamboat Willie* and remained the chief "heavy" for several years until he outlived his usefulness. They were soon joined by an entire menagerie—including the likes of Horace Horsecollar and Clarabelle Cow—but most characters had a relatively short life-span because they proved in-

OPPOSITE: A layout drawing for *Clock Cleaners,* 1937. Layouts like this indicated camera movements and served as a guide for animators and background artists.

capable of development. Pluto made his first tentative appearance as a half-witted bloodhound in a 1930 picture titled *The Chain Gang,* but did not become a distinctive character until gagman Webb Smith and animator Norm Ferguson devised some original "business" for him nearly four years later. Goofy also evolved from a secondary character, originally named Dippy Dawg, but Donald Duck, who first appeared in 1934, catapulted to fame overnight.

Mickey's later entourage included, along with Minnie and Pluto, two mischievous nephews; Donald was joined by Daisy and three nephews of his own—the irrepressible Huey, Dewey, and Louie. Later, he was the victim of many encounters with Chip and Dale, a pair of energetic chipmunks. Other characters, such as the operatic Clara Cluck, made occasional guest appearances.

In many ways, the Mickey Mouse cartoons had much the same impact in the sound era that Mack Sennett and Charlie Chaplin comedies had had in the early years of the American cinema, and Mickey was a decidedly Chaplinesque character in many ways. (As a boy in Kansas City, Disney had admired Chaplin tremendously, often impersonating him in amateur talent contests.) At the outset of his career, it's true, Mickey was sometimes rather callous, often displaying considerable cruelty toward lesser creatures—as, for example, in *Steamboat Willie,* where he and Minnie go to painful lengths to transform a cargo of farm animals into an orchestra. Quite quickly, however, thanks in part to pressure from PTA groups and other concerned citizens worried about the influence this kind of thing was having on children, Mickey mellowed and it was then that he began to acquire some of Chaplin's vulnerability. After this, he became the little man, beset by problems that at first seemed larger than himself but which he invariably overcame.

One advantage that Mickey enjoyed over Chaplin's tramp was that, thanks to the animation medium in which anything is possible, he could enjoy an unfettered fantasy life. In his very first outing, *Plane Crazy,* he imagined himself to be the great hero of the hour, "Lucky" Lindbergh, and built for himself a barnyard contraption of a plane which in no way resembled "The Spirit of St. Louis" but which proved

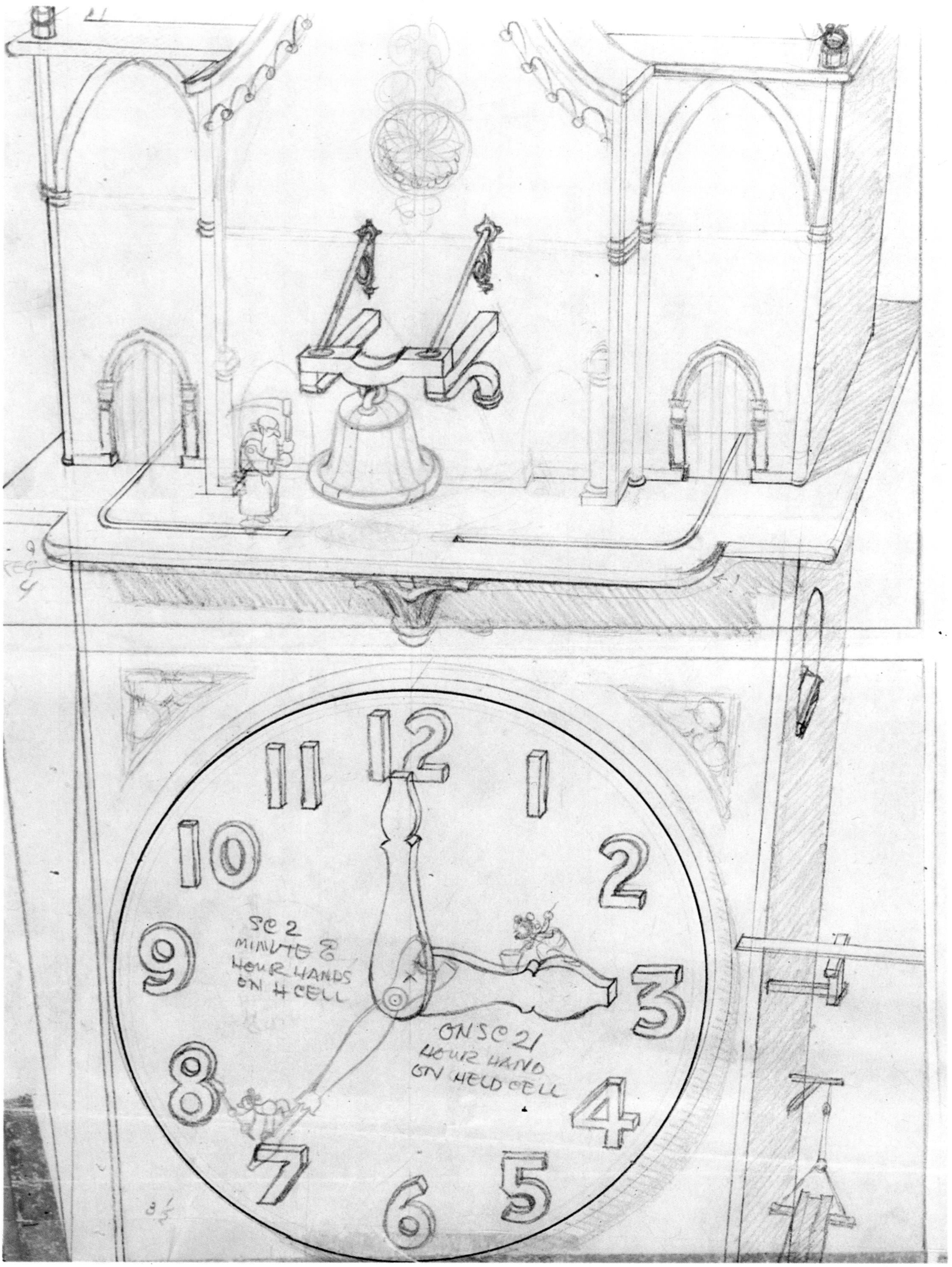

SC 2
MINUTE &
HOUR HANDS
ON 4 CELL

ON SC 21
HOUR HAND
ON HELD CELL

A background painting for *Magician Mickey,* 1937.

capable of performing spectacular, if unpredictable, aerobatics. The infinite flexibility of the medium allowed Mickey to become a jazz pianist, a concert violinist, a football great, or anything else he chose to be. In *Thru the Mirror* he manages a suave impersonation of Fred Astaire. (The Lewis Carroll-like antilogic of this cartoon makes it especially convincing as an animated "dream.") In another short, *Mickey's Premiere,* recognition is given to the fact that Mickey himself has become an authentic movie star as his comedic peers, such as Chaplin, Jimmy Durante, and the Marx Brothers, honor him at a gala premiere. Occasionally Mickey found himself inhabiting fairy tales and children's classics, taking on the role of Gulliver in *Gulliver Mickey* (this film is specifically presented as a dream with Mickey falling asleep and leaving his own body), or Jack in *Jack and the Beanstalk* (transformed into *Mickey and the Beanstock). Fantasia* was built around the episode which presents Mickey as the sorcerer's apprentice.

More often, though, Mickey is back in the everyday world that is his natural environment. He is a grocery boy, he runs a gas station, or he is planning a picnic. Given that Mickey was a product of the Depression, he lives modestly and, in at least one instance, *Moving Day,* he is about to be evicted for failing to pay his rent. As the Disney organization became a little more successful, more "respectable," so did Mickey. He began to dress in a style that suggested a hint of modest affluence. His house seemed a little bigger, a little more comfortably furnished.

"The life and adventures of Mickey Mouse have been closely bound up with my own personal and professional life," Walt Disney once said. "It is understandable that I should have a sentimental attachment for the little personage who played so big a part in the course of Disney Productions and has been so happily accepted as an amusing friend wherever films are shown around the world. He still speaks for me and I still speak for him."

A layout drawing for *Thru the Mirror*, a 1936 Mickey Mouse cartoon.

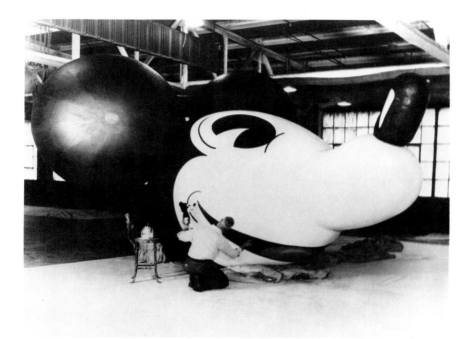

Mickey is prepared for his debut in Macy's Thanksgiving Day parade, 1934.

OPPOSITE: Layouts for *Thru the Mirror,* 1936.

Walt and Mickey were, after all, products of the same environment. Walt loved Mickey—he secretly kept the story sketches for *Steamboat Willie* in his desk—with a special affection he could not quite share with any of his other characters. There were probably practical reasons for his becoming the voice of Mickey. Other people did try out, but Walt knew exactly what he wanted and seems to have been dissatisfied with the others who auditioned. Also, having so recently lost Oswald, the Lucky Rabbit, he was undoubtedly anxious to be sure that no part of Mickey could be stolen from him. Suppose a rival producer had been able to seduce Mickey's voice away? None the less, it must be assumed that the fact that Walt *literally* spoke for Mickey—until, in the late forties, Walt's voice began to thicken and sound effects man Jim MacDonald took over—is of some symbolic significance. If nothing else, it meant that he had to throw himself into the situations that were provided for Mickey. Thus he may well have had a special interest in devising these situations, even at a later date when he was concerned with feature films and other projects.

Evidently we should view Mickey as not just a surrogate for a human type, but as a surrogate for Walt Disney himself. As the tramp was Chaplin's public persona, so Mickey Mouse was Disney's public persona—and the significance of this is inescapa-

A background painting for *The Brave Little Tailor,* 1938.

<small>OPPOSITE:</small> Pluto often found himself bewildered by the world.

ble. Mickey is an American archetype. Walt did not, of course, plan this—such things cannot be planned—but its importance could not have escaped him. As the man behind the archetype, he had to assume a certain responsibility. A sizeable chunk of American mythology had been entrusted to him.

The symbolic relationship between Mickey and Walt Disney continued from 1928 until Mickey's final screen appearance in 1953. Interestingly, it was in the following year that Disney began to make his weekly television appearances. It was as if Mickey had suddenly emerged from his cocoon and turned into the kindly man in the business suit. Soon after, however, Mickey reappeared, in a new form, at Disneyland, wandering through the park and serving his creator once more, this time as a surrogate host.

Chapter Five
DONALD'S DILEMMAS

Donald Duck in *The Autograph Hound,* 1939.

WHEN MICKEY FIRST APPEARED, the sound track was added to an already existing cartoon, the orchestra conductor and sound-effects men carefully following the action on screen with the help of a bouncing ball system that spelled out the rhythmic accents. These accents would correspond with carefully choreographed visual accents on screen (a footstep might fall on every eighth frame of film, and each eight frames might correspond to one beat of a metronome).

Very quickly, however, it was discovered that there was a considerable advantage to creating major parts of the sound track—especially the dialogue—in advance, so that the animators could match their drawings to something that already had a

Clarence Nash, the voice of Donald Duck.

OPPOSITE: Sketches from a Donald Duck story board.

FOLLOWING PAGES: A background painting for *Donald's Lucky Day,* 1939.

physical existence. Thus many Disney characters crystallized around "voice talents," the actors who provided the cartoon creatures with the power of speech. The character of Sneezy in *Snow White,* for example, developed from a routine Disney had heard comedian Billy Gilbert perform on radio and in vaudeville.

A few years earlier, in 1933 or 1934, Disney first heard a man called Clarence Nash. Nash was employed, at the time, by a Southern California dairy which used him in a public-relations capacity. His claim to fame was that he did "funny voices" and extraordinarily lifelike animal imitations. (He was apt to enter a room with a snort like that of a nervous stallion.) The dairy found that these talents amused children, and children drank a lot of milk.

It has been said that Disney first heard Nash on the radio, though old-timers recall that Nash would visit the old Disney studio on Hyperion Avenue in Silver Lake aboard one of the dairy's delivery trucks. In any case, Disney and various members of his animation staff heard what Nash could do and came to the conclusion that he might be useful to them as a voice talent. There was one "funny voice" in particular that fascinated them, but no one was quite sure what to do with it. Attempts were made to match all kinds of animals, from alligators to zebras, with this voice—Nash made it with his lips held together and pockets of air in his

Later, of course, he also developed a strong line in paranoia. The entire world seemed to conspire against him. He remained, in a sense, a victim of the Depression long after it was over. In his relatively prosperous later years—I predicate this prosperity on the changes in his surroundings—he could never adjust to the possibility of good fortune. If circumstances did not provide him with a ready-made crisis to awaken his rage, then he would precipitate one by antagonizing some innocent bystander.

In all fairness to the embattled Duck, Disney did provide him with more than his fair share of ongoing trouble when he introduced Huey, Dewey, and Louie into Donald's life. These anarchistic nephews can be seen as a kind of personification of the wildest aspects of childhood. Donald, on the other hand, represents the adult world at its intolerant worst. What makes this confrontation tragic as well as hilarious is the realization that Donald must once have been exactly like his nephews, and that they are destined to become like him. His ability to antagonize has its roots in the kind of mischievousness that they thrive on, and their vulnerability to criticism—their egos are easily bruised—will probably bloom one day into full-fledged paranoia.

Donald is a type that might be found in any culture—an adult who has never grown up emotionally, who wants to be loved but is not really capable of loving in return—but he remains in many particulars a product of Depression America. By giving the American public the opportunity to laugh at the Duck, Walt Disney may have performed an important purgative service, acting as a kind of exorcist.

Chapter Six
THE GOOF

Goofy as a jitterbug. Sketch for an unused segment of *Make Mine Music.*

Goofy—INVARIABLY REFERRED TO by Disney veterans as "the Goof"—is a twentieth-century descendant of the village idiot. One might think that this would make him an unlikely candidate for stardom but, in fact, the Goof, once his character had become clearly defined, was found to provide the Disney artists with a bottomless well of situations and eventually graduated to his own series of cartoon shorts.

Goofy, bumbling through life to the tune of "The World Owes Me a Living," is an irresistibly likable character, a divine innocent. There is not a malicious bone in his lanky body. Anatomically he is a kind of dog-faced man, which makes him ideal for situations in which human physical aspirations are to be parodied. If you wanted to

105

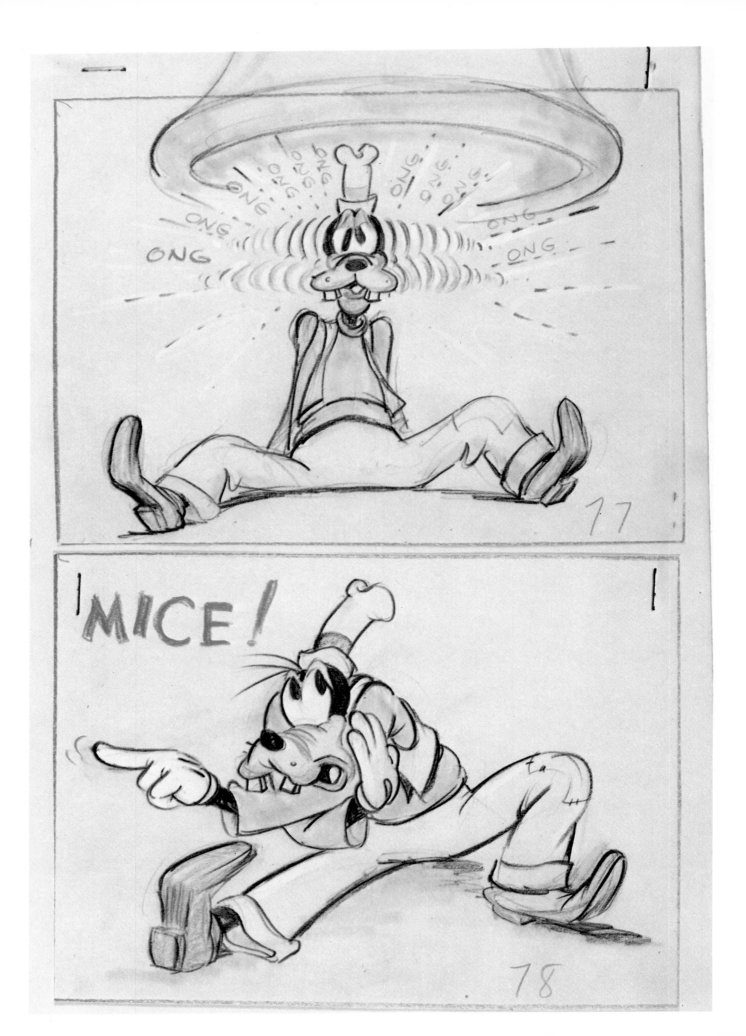

Pinto Colvig, the voice of Goofy and also a top Disney gag man.

OPPOSITE: Story sketches for *Clock Cleaners,* 1937.

make a cartoon about a greenhorn learning to ride a horse, then Goofy is the character that you would turn to since his physique is precisely that of an uncoordinated human. Also, his face is wonderfully expressive. His thought processes are so slow and so close to the surface that every painful step of his efforts to make logical sense of the world, to relate cause to effect, is registered in his eyes and in the furrows of his brows. This makes him an animator's dream.

Since Goofy evolved slowly from Dippy Dawg, no one person can be said to have created him. To a large extent, he developed around the voice of Pinto Colvig, a gagman who also provided him with many good story situations, and old-timers point to Art Babbitt as the animator who first understood the Goof's full potential.

In his ridiculous battered hat and jaunty vest, Goofy was first used as a foil for Mickey and Donald. In many of the best shorts of the mid- and late thirties, they appeared as a trio. In cartoons such as *Clock Cleaners* and *Moving Day*—almost faultless examples of the early Disney idiom—these three characters were used to ring every possible change on a given situation. Each was so different from the others, and yet they complemented one another perfectly. Goofy's amiable imbecility—his lack of comprehension when faced with, for example, the simple consequences of the laws of gravity—could be counted on to get the friends into trouble. Donald's irascibility would inevitably make things worse while Mickey, however much the odds were stacked against him by comrades and circumstances, would generally manage to save the day. Mickey's cheerful optimism might have become cloying if it had not been for Donald's capacity for rage, and Donald's rage might have become tiresome had it not been neutralized by Goofy's good-natured bungling.

It would be wonderful if this generation could have a chance to see these thirties cartoons again—they are seldom shown in theaters today—since they are among the finest work Disney ever produced. It was these brief but densely packed master-pieces that prompted people as varied as H.G. Welles, Thornton Wilder, and Rene Clair to declare that Walt Disney was one of the undisputed geniuses of the cinema. These cartoons were not quite like anything else that had preceeded them. Even the great comedy shorts of the silent era did not achieve quite the same blend of outrageous invention and tight control. In a word, the Disney cartoons are unique.

Later, Goofy was utilized as a solo performer in a series of shorts that satirized a wide variety of human vanities and foibles. He demonstrated the noble art of self-defense, he attempted to give up smoking, and he learned, after many mishaps, to drive on the freeway. His innate inability to comprehend the simplest set of instructions guaranteed disaster at every step, and his unfailing good humor permitted him to face embarrassment with unexpected dignity.

It was, though, in the cartoons of the mid-thirties that Goofy, along with Mickey and Donald, was seen at his best. Taken as a whole, Disney's earlier short cartoons—more than two hundred were released between 1928 and Pearl Harbor—constitute a fascinating anthology of American attitudes of the period. Each of them is an image of American society seen through the refracting lens of the cartoonist's imagination. In the great majority of them, most members of the audience would recognize some situation or character they could identify with, something that related to their own experience of life. Whereas many Hollywood pictures of the period—let us recall, for example, those vehicles that were built around stars like Garbo and Dietrich—entertained by taking the audience into areas of ex-

Sketches for How To Ride a Horse, originally released as part of *The Reluctant Dragon,* 1941.

OPPOSITE: Goofy in scenes from a 1937 short, *Mickey's Amateurs* (top), and from *Saludos Amigos,* 1943.

A layout drawing showing the interior of the clocktower in *Clock Cleaners*. By some oversight, the artist has neglected to reverse the numbers in the clock face. From this viewpoint we should be seeing them from behind.

OPPOSITE: Story sketches for *Cleaners*.

perience that were a million miles from the everyday, most of Disney's shorts capitalized on the magic of the ordinary, picking up on common situations and magnifying them into miniature epics of comic invention.

Along with a handful of other masters such as W.C. Fields, the Marx Brothers, Chaplin, Laurel and Hardy, and the great radio comedians, Disney provided America with a vital commodity, a humorous commentary on the decade of the Great Depression. Disney's shorts rendered the absurd palatable by making it entertaining. His homespun brand of comedy was liberating and never cynical. It was a tonic that arrived on the scene when America needed it most.

Chapter Seven
BACK ON MAIN STREET

Make Mine Music, 1946.

WHEN WALT DISNEY WAS WORKING on his first great features—*Snow White, Pinocchio, Fantasia, Dumbo, Bambi*—his obvious involvement with Main Street U.S.A. diminished for a while (though the values of Main Street continued to inform these pictures). In the years following World War II, however, the Disney studio turned back to small-town America as a direct source of inspiration.

In the early years, Walt Disney had had an easy rapport with the American public. He seemed to understand instinctively what people wanted to see on screen; his taste and the public's were one and the same. Success and corporate growth, however, threatened that happy state of affairs.

It was not that Disney was spoiled by success—he was not the kind of man to be over-impressed by his own celebrity—but it did create certain problems. As his organization became larger, he was forced to delegate more responsibility and this meant he could no longer fly by the seat of his pants, and thus could not exercise his intuition so freely. We should recognize, too, that part of Disney's rapport with

AT RIGHT, OPPOSITE AND PRECEDING PAGES:
Scenes from "All the Cats Join In,"
a segment of the 1946 release
Make Mine Music. This portion of
the film was animated to the music
of Benny Goodman.

the public in the early days had sprung from the fact that he was perceived as standing outside the Hollywood establishment. Alongside giants like Paramount and Twentieth Century-Fox, the Disney studio was a nickel-and-dime operation. It was as if a dry-goods store was attempting to compete with Macy's and Gimbels, and everyone loves a David-and-Goliath confrontation. Later, however, the Disney studio itself became part of the establishment and so no longer had an automatic guarantee of public sympathy.

In the early days, decisions had almost made themselves, but that was no longer the case in the postwar world. The nation was changing rapidly. The common cause of the Depression and the war years soon disintegrated under the pressure of swelling affluence. Hollywood, inevitably, reflected this. In the films of the thirties and early forties, the viewer generally knew exactly where he stood—good and evil were clearly delineated so it was difficult to find oneself rooting for the wrong side. From the mid-forties on, the differences between good and evil became somewhat clouded. A star like Humphrey Bogart always did the right thing in the end, but his screen persona was essentially amoral. A typical Bogart character of the late forties had been in the war, had done his bit for democracy, and now wanted to settle down to making a fast few bucks without bothering with ideological problems and without caring too much whom he worked for.

The values in Hollywood movies became blurred largely because the market was no longer as clear-cut as it had been. It was slowly disintegrating into many markets. In the thirties, people had gone to see almost anything, confident that they would be entertained by whatever MGM or RKO cared to provide for them that week. Now, increasingly, musicals and romances drew one audience, war stories and Westerns another, horror movies a third, and so on. The genres became more defined, then all too often caricatured, as producers wooed not the public but this or that *sector* of the public. The advent of television, soon to become the chief purveyor of mainstream entertainment, exaggerated this trend still further. Walt Disney, in common with other studio heads, had to make up his mind just what constituted his potential audience.

Consciously or unconsciously, Disney decided that his market was the American family, which was, in fact, the surviving vestige of the old Hollywood general market. His films would not be geared to courting couples in drive-ins, or to housewives looking for a good cry. They would be intended for parents and children, family units who wanted an inexpensive evening out together. His decision must, of course, have been guided by what he knew he could do best. Animation had lent itself very well to the old, clear-cut values—to simple confrontations between archetypal heroes and villains—and to a basic kind of broad comedy that

119

Scenes from "Casey at the Bat," another segment of *Make Mine Music*.

FOLLOWING PAGES: *Lady and the Tramp*, 1955.

An early study for a scene in *Lady and the Tramp,* the first animated feature to be made in Cinemascope.

AT LEFT AND OPPOSITE: Scenes from *Lady and the Tramp*.

had been around since Mack Sennett unleashed the Keystone Kops on the movie-going public. Even when he moved into live-action film making, and other fields of entertainment, Disney seldom strayed far from his tried-and-true idioms.

It can be argued that this made many of his later films relatively synthetic, and it's true that he was seldom able to recapture the spontaneity, the sheer joy and excitement of discovery, that marked the best shorts and features of the thirties and early forties. A number of fine pictures—*Cinderella, Lady and the Tramp, Treasure Island, 20,000 Leagues Under the Sea, Mary Poppins*—were made at the studio after 1945; but the old innocence, the old daredevil quality, had vanished.

So, the values remained the same but there was a substantial difference in tone. What had been taken for granted before was now used in a very deliberate way. Two segments of *Make Mine Music*, released in 1946, were in some respects the harbingers of things to come. "All the Cats Join In" dealt with a contemporary aspect of Main Street. To the music of the Benny Goodman Quartet, teenagers enacted the rituals of hot rod and soda fountain, juke box and jitterbug. The animation of the segment was imaginative, the tone mildly satirical, and this kind of updated Main Street theme can be seen as prefiguring certain live-action comedies of the fifties and sixties—*The Shaggy Dog, The Absent Minded Professor, Son of Flubber, The Misadventures of Merlin Jones*—in which the likes of Fred MacMurray, Annette Funicello, and Tommy Kirk encountered unlikely events in small-town settings. Often these small towns were also college towns so that these pictures recall the campus comedies of the thirties in which such stars as Bing Crosby and Jack Oakie masqueraded as the eternal student.

The other segment of *Make Mine Music* to deal with a Main Street theme was "Casey at the Bat," which is a comic gloss on the famous poem—in the movie, the story is told and sung by Jerry Colonna—and anticipates the outright catering to nostalgia that is so common in Disney's later work. In this instance, we are back in America near the turn of the century, and this was to provide the setting for one of Disney's finest postwar animated features, *Lady and the Tramp.*

Scenes from *Lady and the Tramp*.

Peg, the sultry torch singer of the dog pound. A scene from *Lady and the Tramp*.

The unnamed city of *Lady and the Tramp* is bigger, certainly, than the Mudville of "Casey at the Bat." It appears to be an affluent, growing community, but it is small enough to retain the atmosphere of Main Street. This picture, released in 1955, was the first animated feature to be made in Cinemascope. The story concerns dogs and their interaction with the human world. Stylistically it is naturalistic. Lady, Tramp, Jock, Trusty, Peg, and their canine friends reflect human society but they look and behave like real dogs. The settings are charmingly evoked and look, at times, like architects' renderings for Disneyland's Main Street. That Main Street was, of course, being built while *Lady and the Tramp* was in production, and a degree of cross-pollination was perhaps inevitable.

It seems to have been at about this point, then, in the mid-fifties, that Walt Disney returned definitively to his roots which he had, in any case, never left far behind.

PART TWO

Past, Present and Future:

is the Hall of Presidents where, at frequent intervals, Lincoln delivers a moving
speech to an ever-changing audience and with the evident approval of his assembled peers.

Liberty Square is another example of tasteful and charming period reconstruction—a kind of miniature Williamsburg—an imaginary township of the revolutionary era combining elements of Dutch and British colonial architecture. Like
Main Street, Liberty Square is too well maintained, too clean, to seem like part of
any real world—the way the Florida sun beats down on the pastel-colored walls
tends to emphasize this—but the craftsmanship is authentic enough, and the environment created here is true to the myth, and it was the myth that always
fascinated Disney.

New Orleans Square in Disneyland, with its wrought-iron balconies and curved
terraces, its graceful stairways and hanging vines, is perhaps the most delightful of
all the period reconstructions in the parks. Again, the ambiance is far removed
from that of its model—the French Quarter in New Orleans—but the sheer elegance
of the architecture is stunning and, like every corner of Disneyland, it has acquired
an atmosphere of its own.

On film, Disney had begun to deal with American historical themes, drawn from
both fact and fiction, soon after World War II. Two animated examples are
"Johnny Appleseed," a segment of *Melody Time* released in 1948, and "Ichabod
Crane," the first half of *Ichabod and Mr. Toad*, which appeared the following year.
"Johnny Appleseed" tells the story of the folklore hero, who is said to have brought
the apple tree to the West, in broad cartoonist's strokes that are more vigorous
than subtle. In "Ichabod," Washington Irving's ludicrous schoolmaster is dealt with
in terms of caricature, but the essential lines of the story are retained and the plot
moves steadily and inevitably toward its terrifying ending. The way in which comedy and horror are played off against one another at the climax of "Ichabod" makes
for perhaps the most frightening sequence in all of Disney's movies.

In live-action films, Disney dealt with several different periods of American

136

"Johnny Appleseed," a segment of the 1948 release *Melody Time.*

OPPOSITE: *New Orleans Square.*

history. *The Light in the Forest* (1956) is a story of colonial days and the relationship between Indians and settlers, while *Johnny Tremain* (1957) is set during the Revolutionary War, and *The Great Locomotive Chase* (1956) dramatizes an incident from the Civil War. The vast majority of Disney's historical films, however, concerned themselves with various phases of the opening up of the American West, or with the settled rural world that came into being as the frontier moved ever closer to the Pacific Ocean.

*   *   *

From the beginning, Mickey and his friends occasionally parodied the conventions of the Hollywood Western and, in *Melody Time,* Roy Rogers narrated the animated story of Pecos Bill—an amusing exploration of a well-known folk myth. For the most part, though, Disney animators steered clear of the frontier as a source of subject matter and left it to their co-workers in the live-action field. It was really with his advent as a television producer that Disney began to turn to the Old West as a major theme in his work.

The Disneyland television series debuted on October 17, 1954, several months before the park itself, and enjoyed its most spectacular success just seven weeks later with the airing of *Davy Crockett, Indian Fighter.* Subsequent episodes—

139

Scenes from *Ichabod,* 1948.

Davy Crockett, first shown in 1954.

shown in January and February of 1955—took Davy Crockett (played by Fess Parker) to the halls of Congress and, finally, to his death at the Alamo. So enthusiastic was the reception of these shows, which were produced by Bill Walsh and directed by Norman Foster, that they were edited into a theatrical feature which was released in the summer of 1955. Later, Davy was resurrected for two further episodes, *Davy Crockett's Keel Boat Race* and *Davy Crockett and the River Pirates,* which also provided the basis for a theatrical release. Meanwhile, the theme song written for the original three-part series—"The Ballad of Davy Crockett"—had become a smash hit, and kids all over the country were sporting coonskin hats.

Hollywood had long exploited the myth of the frontier in the form of the Western. From the days of Broncho Billy Anderson and William S. Hart, the hero in the white hat had pursued the bad guys across the slopes of the Santa Monica Mountains and through the canyons of the Simi Hills. For the most part, movie and television producers have concentrated on the latter phases of the opening of the West—on the age of the gunfighter and the frontier saloon, of Matt Dillon and Billy the Kid. Davy Crockett's earliest adventures remind us, however, of a period when land east of the Mississippi was still being settled. (Crockett's native state, Tennessee, was not admitted to the Union until 1796, when he was ten years old.) This was fresh material and the public responded to it, as did the management of ABC, which demanded more of the same thing. Disney gave them Texas John Slaughter (Tom Tryon), Elfego Baca (Robert Loggia), and even revived the character of Zorro for a series starring Guy Williams. Most of these shows did well, but Disney was not satisfied with the situation. He disliked being asked to repeat old successes—finding the idea both boring and pointless—and disdained being typecast as competition for *Wyatt Earp* and *Maverick.* This seems to have been a major factor in his decision to move his television activities to the NBC network for the 1961-62 season.

In the Davy Crockett episodes, however, and in some other shows, he had brought to the screen his own vision of the opening of America, and it had its own distinctive flavor. Feature films such as *Ten Who Dared* and *Tonka* amplified this.

Pastel Sketches for "Pecos Bill,"
a segment of *Melody Time.*

FOLLOWING PAGES: *Song of the South,* 1946.

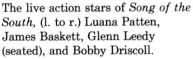
The live action stars of *Song of the South,* (l. to r.) Luana Patten, James Baskett, Glenn Leedy (seated), and Bobby Driscoll.

Disney was, by Hollywood standards, early in treating American Indians as noble beings rather than as painted savages. In *Tonka*, for example—starring Sal Mineo and released in 1958—General Custer is portrayed as a genocidal maniac while the Indians, except for one unpleasant character, are essentially brave and dignified. Most Hollywood Westerns have refined the formulae that were developed in the pulp fictions and the stage melodramas of the late nineteenth century. Disney, by contrast, seems to owe more to the tradition that began with *The Last of the Mohicans.* His version of the Western—with the exception of the Zorro series—was surprisingly naturalistic. The plots are simplified, but they generally have some kind of historical basis.

Disney was fascinated by the pioneers and by the native Americans they encountered as they settled in the wilderness, but he was equally enchanted with the world of their immediate heirs—the America that saw homesteads replaced by

The Brer Rabbit sequences of *Song of the South* featured some of the best animation to come out of the Disney studio since before the war.

In "The Martins and the Coys," a
segment of *Make Mine Music,*
Disney gave the public a hillbilly
version of *Romeo and Juliet.*

farms and embryonic cities, and canoes replaced by paddle-wheelers—by the beginnings of civilization in the heartland where he had spent his boyhood. These two phases of the settling of the West are juxtaposed in the Frontierland sections of the theme parks. The riverboat *Mark Twain* docks near trading posts and stockades that belong to an earlier era. History is telescoped so that the early growth of America is condensed into a compact panorama that can be absorbed at a glance.

Disney's own experience of rural America had surfaced many times in the early Mickey Mouse cartoons—titles such as *Barnyard Olympics* abound. In these shorts, the farm offered a fertile proving ground for the imagination of Disney artists. Stables could become broadcasting studios, agricultural implements could be transformed into musical instruments, and the barnyard, of course, was the natural habitat of the animal characters who populated these cartoons. As the characters acquired more and more human habits, however, the farm setting was used less frequently.

Rural America reappeared after the war in two important movies, *Song of the South* (1946) and *So Dear to My Heart* (1948). Starring James Baskett along with Bobby Driscoll and Luana Patten, *Song of the South* was a live-action film with animated segments in which the Uncle Remus stories were brought to life. The live-action sequences evoked the rural South and the animated portions dealt with its folklore. At some points—notably the famous "Zip-a-dee Doo-Dah" number—live action and animation were marvelously combined to provide a transition between the world of reality and the world of myth.

So Dear to My Heart—also starring Bobby Driscoll and Luana Patten, this time along with Burl Ives—is primarily the story of a young boy's devotion to his pet sheep. It conjures up the world of farm life and county fairs in the early years of the century and can best be described as a modest but beautifully sustained exercise in nostalgia. Whether it bore any relation to Walt Disney's own boyhood experiences on the farm in Missouri is open to speculation. Clearly, though, it is the way he wanted to remember things.

149

Chapter Nine
THE WILDERNESS

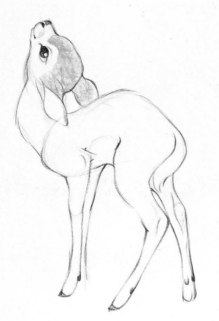

A sketch for *Bambi,* 1942.
FOLLOWING PAGES: Bambi and his mother.

ONE OF THE MOST REMARKABLE PARTS of Walt Disney World is never seen by the general public. This is a carefully protected nature preserve, 7,500 acres of cypress swamp—a tangle of vines, hardwood trees and underbrush, alive with alligators, water snakes, deer, exotic birds, and the last Florida black bear—the only remaining tract of untouched wilderness in central Florida. Except for the resident team of scientists, few people ever enter this preserve, which constitutes almost a third of the area occupied by Walt Disney World. (Much of the rest is given over to nature trails, some of them quite wild in themselves.) This preserve was part of Disney's plan from the very outset and it reflects his long-standing interest in nature, an interest which first appeared in his work with *Bambi.*

Preliminary work on *Bambi* began as early as the end of 1937, immediately after the completion of *Snow White,* but—although a skeleton crew continued to develop the idea—it was shelved temporarily as *Pinocchio* and *Fantasia* stretched the studio's manpower and resources to the limit. With *Fantasia* finished, *Bambi* went

back into full production and was eventually released in August, 1942.

Adapted from Felix Salten's popular book, *Bambi* was a project close to Walt Disney's heart, and he was determined to spare no effort in bringing it to the screen. Special art classes, taught by Rico Le Brun, were instituted, and thousands of studies were made of animal anatomy and locomotion. Still photographers and movie cameramen were sent out into the wild to record animals in their natural habitat, and two deer were installed at the studio as live models.

The art direction team, under Tom Codrick, and the background stylists, headed by Tyrus Wong, went to great pains to create a forest environment that would itself be, in effect, a character in the story. The moods of nature and the cycle of the seasons are as important to *Bambi* as anything that happens to the animals who live in the forest. These animals were animated by a hand-picked group that included many of the most gifted younger artists.

Salten's book is set in a European forest, but the film version is clearly informed by the artists' response to the American wilderness—this might be Maine or northern Minnesota. It is the world in which the American Indian was at home and which was later explored by trappers and pioneers.

Scene by scene, *Bambi* is a splendid, technically innovative film. All of the studio's ingenuity was brought to bear upon sustaining its lyrical mood, rare in the world of animation, and on creating convincing animal characters who were not, for once, strictly human surrogates. And yet their psychology is a little too human. Bambi's reaction to the death of his mother is a mirror of human emotion, and Thumper's sense of mischief is exactly that of a small boy. (He is also permitted to consort with an owl who, in the real wild, would make short work of him.) It is not that the animator should be forbidden to take such liberties, but in this story man is supposed to be the enemy—the greatest predator of all—yet the wild creatures often think and talk like men, which tends to blunt the moral of the picture.

The internal evidence of the film suggests that the studio's artists would have been capable of making a movie that relied solely on the accurate observation of nature, a movie that would have told its story without dialogue, without gags, but

An enormous amount of preliminary work went into the making of *Bambi,* and thousands of atmospheric sketches, such as these pastel studies, were made.

FOLLOWING PAGES: Winter in the forest.

THIS PAGE AND OPPOSITE: Scenes from *Bambi*.
FOLLOWING PAGES: *The Living Desert,* 1953.

The Vanishing Prairie, 1954.

Disney apparently did not feel that such a picture would find a large enough audience to justify its cost of well over two million dollars, a huge investment for that time. In one respect, then, the film is a compromise, but Walt's sense of what his audience would accept was borne out by the picture's success, and the film's shortcomings need not be allowed to destroy the pleasure we receive from its many brilliant passages.

A few years later, Disney began to think about the possibility of making a film of the last American frontier—Alaska. He began to research the potential that existed there by hiring two 16mm film buffs, Al and Elma Milotte, residents of the territory, to travel about Alaska shooting material that might suggest some idea to the Disney story department. They sent back footage of eskimos and miners, hydroelectric plants and highway projects—all of which was shelved until the first reels began to arrive from the Milottes' expedition to the Pribilof Islands, isolated rocks in the Bering Sea where fur seals gather each year to mate and raise their young. When Disney saw this material, he realized that here was a tremendous primaeval drama which nobody but naturalists had ever seen. The fierce battles between the gigantic bull seals and the education of the pups gave the film that

166

Beaver Valley, 1950.

was put together a kind of elemental quality. The problem was that no distributor was interested in it. Disney solved this problem by forming his own distribution company, Buena Vista, and booking *Seal Island* into a Los Angeles theater for two weeks so that it would be eligible for an Academy Award nomination. It was not only nominated but also won the Oscar for best short subject of the year, which gave it the impetus it needed when it went into general release. We take this kind of film for granted now—television is saturated with nature documentaries—but at the time it appeared, in 1949, *Seal Island* was a complete novelty for the general public and enjoyed a striking success.

This led to a number of similar pictures, the so-called True Life Adventure series, both short subjects—*Bear Country, Beaver Valley, The Olympic Elk, Nature's Half Acre*—and full-length features such as *White Wilderness, The Living Desert,* and *The Vanishing Prairie.* Many, especially the last two named, were fascinating evocations of untouched America.

Out of these documentaries evolved another kind of nature film—part documentary, part drama—in which both wild and trained animals were used to conjure up adventures in wilderness settings. Good examples of the genre are *Nikki, Wild Dog of the North* (1961) and *The Legend of Lobo* (1962), and a number of similar vehicles were produced for the Disney television show.

167

FOLLOWING PAGES: A scene from *Water Birds.*

Chapter Ten
WARTIME

Donald Get's Drafted, 1942.

Throughout his career, Walt Disney turned to America for inspiration, drawing on its history, folklore, and landscape. During World War II, however, America turned to him—as it did to the movie industry as a whole—to make a contribution to the war effort and to help maintain civilian morale.

The early days of the war were difficult for the Disney studio. Key personnel entered the services and material shortages meant a partial curtailment of production. For a while, the studio was even required to accommodate an anti-aircraft unit consisting of seven hundred men with all their guns and equipment.

Production did continue, however, and one result of the war was a brief renaissance of the short cartoon. For several years, feature films had had priority as far as the studio's top artists were concerned (though many of them liked to work on a short, from time to time, as a change of pace). After *Dumbo* and *Bambi,* some of the most gifted animators again found themselves assigned to work on shorts. Wartime cartoons such as *Victory Vehicles* and *Commando Duck* made

During the war years, the Disney studio did all kinds of work for the government and for the armed services. Disney artists made training films, designed posters to help the war effort, and contributed cartoons to service newspapers and periodicals.

On these pages we see examples of the many insignia that the studio designed for various military units. These insignia appeared in all theaters of the war, painted onto the sides of bombers, fighters, tanks, jeeps and every imaginable kind of vehicle.

Disney's satirical view of Hitler's Germany.
A sketch for *Der Fuehrer's Face,* 1943.

imaginative use of material presented by the war—material drawn from both the armed services and the home front. Other shorts, like *Education for Death* and *Der Fuehrer's Face,* were hilarious anti-Nazi propaganda vehicles.

In 1941, Disney made a State Department sponsored trip to South America, and this resulted in a forty-three-minute film called *Saludos Amigos,* aimed in part at creating goodwill in the Latin countries, the war in Europe having cut off the American film industry from many of its established export markets. *Saludos Amigos* is a "package" film, consisting of four short cartoons set in a travelogue montaged from footage of the Disney party in Peru, Chile, Argentina, and Brazil. The first animated segment presents Donald Duck as a typical American tourist visiting Lake Titicaca. The second is the story of Pedro, the little mail plane, and his adventures amidst the Andes. In the third, Goofy demonstrates what it takes to be a brave gaucho of the Argentinian pampas, while, in the final animated segment, Donald shows up at the carnival in Rio de Janeiro and is taken in hand by a new Disney character, José Carioca.

Saludos Amigos was followed, in 1945, by a more ambitious package film, *The*

174

Another sardonic vision of the Nazi landscape
from *Der Fuehrer's Face.*

Three Caballeros, in which Donald and José Carioca were joined by Panchito, a Mexican rooster with an itchy trigger finger. This movie involved more Latin American adventures and even saw Donald falling in love with Aurora Miranda, sister of the more famous Carmen Miranda. It cannot be counted as one of Disney's greatest pictures, but it is full of high spirits and surrealistic sight gags.

Meanwhile, the Disney studio was also working for the government and the armed services, making animated training films and educational shorts. These were remarkable in that they were of necessity made very cheaply and pioneered many so-called limited animation techniques—in effect, short cuts that avoided the laborious work that went into the standard Disney cartoon.

Related to these, though produced at Disney's own expense, was a sixty-five-minute feature called *Victory Through Air Power,* which expounded the strategic bombing theories of Major Alexander de Seversky, theories that were later put into effect by allied air forces in their raids on Hitler's Germany. The studio also contributed war posters, illustrations for service magazines, insignia for aircraft and military units, and generally attempted to satisfy any request that might help the war effort.

175

Three Caballeros united Donald Duck with José Carioca,
a Brazilian parrot, Panchito, a gun toting Mexican
rooster, and a bevy of Latin American beauties.

Chapter Eleven
NOSTALGIA FOR THE FUTURE

The Walt Disney World monorail with Space Mountain in the background.

WALT DISNEY WAS ALWAYS COMFORTABLE with the past. He turned to it naturally, as to an old friend. The future, I suspect, was something he came upon almost by accident. At first, he approached it cautiously, but soon he became infatuated with it and, toward the end of his life, the possibilities it offered became his consuming passion.

Like many American boys of his generation, he had always been attracted to novelty and the latest gadgets. As remarked earlier, his romance with the technical side of animation—his sense of helping a form of expression develop from a primitive state by the refinement of mechanical devices until they could match the potential of his artists—was crucial to his success. He was always ready to embrace the latest developments, whether they were the multiplane camera or the printed circuits and servomechanisms that control the audio-animatronic figures who people the Haunted Mansions and other attractions at the parks. But such pragmatic

Inside Space Mountain.

uses of technology are very different from a concern with the future as an abstraction.

It was really with Tomorrowland that Disney first confronted the idea of the future and its implications for America. In planning Disneyland, he recognized that he must deal with past, present, and future—just as a story has a beginning, a middle, and an end. The future does not have the definitiveness of an ending, however; it is not simply a matter of living happily ever after. It is, rather, a fresh beginning, a fact that seems to have appealed greatly to Disney's imagination. In 1966, he made the following comments:

> **Now, when we opened Disneyland, outer space was Buck Rogers. I did put in a trip to the moon, and I got Wernher von Braun to help me plan the thing. And, of course, we were going up to the moon long before Sputnik. And since then has come Sputnik and then has come our great program in outer space. So I had to tear down my Tomorrowland that I built eleven years ago and rebuild it to keep pace.**

It is one of the paradoxes about Walt Disney that he was able to produce perfectly rounded works of art, like *Snow White,* and yet could possess a positive passion for the unfinished, for the open-ended experience. He loved the parks because they could grow indefinitely, and he came to love the notion of the future because it is like an empty vessel waiting to be filled with new ideas and, ultimately, ideas were his primary stock in trade.

We might say, in fact, that the first half of Disney's career—culminating when he was in his late thirties—was devoted to bringing his own kind of perfection to a specific form, the animated film. In the latter part of his career, he became more and more obsessed with the generation of ideas almost for their own sakes. Having succeeded so completely in his first goal, he was free to indulge in what may come to seem, in retrospect, his most remarkable talent. Ideas were, for him, the stuff of which life is made and—like some figures in the fine arts, people such as John Cage and Robert Rauschenberg—he seems to have become increasingly involved with

OPPOSITE: The Walt Disney World monorail leaves the Polynesian Hotel.

FOLLOWING PAGES: Tomorrowland after dark.

diminishing the gap between art and life. *Snow White* is an entity unto itself—it is something that cannot be acted upon by the viewer, though the viewer can bring much to it. Disneyland and Walt Disney World, on the other hand, are vast entertainment machines that can only be brought to life by the people who use them.

Walt Disney was an inventor. He did not take out patents on a new kind of roller bearing, or an improved internal combustion engine, but he was an inventor nonetheless. He invented unexpected pleasures and new states of mind; he invented truly innocent adventures (a miracle in the latter half of the twentieth century), and uniquely American perspectives on the world. The parks are where all this came to ultimate fruition.

Perhaps the later films suffered because of this. How could Walt Disney be satisfied with the fixed delights of the motion picture when he could enjoy the never-ending pleasure of inventing and re-inventing Disneyland and Walt Disney World? How could he give the same attention to story details when he could let his inspiration roam in the ever-changing structures of the parks? In the history of music or literature, for example, we often find a composer or poet mastering a given form, then going beyond that to create his own universe with a richer and more flexible structure. This is precisely what Disney managed to do in the entertainment field.

Tomorrowland, from the beginning, has been a mixture of science fiction and science fact. There was a side to Disney which liked to mix entertainment with instruction—it is (or was) a classic American attitude that art and entertainment are more palatable if they can be made to serve the purposes of education—thus Tomorrowland's trip to the moon and voyage through the atom were conceived as being vehicles to convey information as well as exciting adventures.

As we have seen, despite his gifts as a fantasist, Disney was essentially a practical man, and thinking about the future gave him an opportunity to exercise this aspect of his character. His love of steam locomotives and horse-drawn trams did not blind him to the fact that the transportation of the future would be radically

182

different. Years before most urban planners were awake to the problems, he confronted the primacy of the need to face up to air pollution and fuel economy. The monorails that run through Disneyland and Walt Disney World are both metaphors for a future society and remarkably clean vehicles in that they do not pump exhaust emissions into the atmosphere. The comically efficient "People Movers" also offer real lessons for the city planners of tomorrow. Powered by a simple friction-drive system, the "People Movers" are fuel efficient and would provide an excellent means of transportation within neighborhoods. Beyond that, they are—with their bulbous body work and perky canopies—essentially lovable. They are, appropriately, like something out of a cartoon and, as was the case with the old-fashioned trolley car, this is the kind of vehicle to which one could become sentimentally attached. The fact that they can move along an elevated track, as they do in the parks, makes them all the more attractive. Valuable ground space can be saved for other purposes—parkland for example—and the rider has the exhilarating experience of riding at rooftop level, enjoying the kind of panoramic view that is seldom available from cars and buses.

The writer Ray Bradbury once proposed that Walt Disney should run for mayor of Los Angeles on the grounds that Disney was possibly the one man alive who could make the city work. Disney declined, saying that he would be a fool to seek the office when he was already the monarch of a Magic Kingdom. One can see his point, but one also understands why Bradbury made the proposal, because Disney's Magic Kingdom was full of down-to-earth ideas that would make a good deal of sense within real urban complexes. And Bradbury is not the only one to have recognized this fact. Just a decade ago, Disneyland was looked on as a mere entertainment area. Today, Disneyland and especially Walt Disney World are objects of pilgrimages for architects and city planners because, in these places, systems that visionaries only dreamed of have become realities and can be observed in operation.

When Disney built Walt Disney World, he wanted to avoid being hemmed in by motels and fast-food franchises (such had been the fate of Disneyland), so he systematically went about acquiring a huge tract—forty-three square miles—in central Florida so that he could develop a truly self-contained complex. Wishing to avoid the ecological damage that had been wrought by conventional drainage and land-fill techniques in much of Florida, he first had the property's water levels regulated by an elaborate system of levees and sluice gates so that certain areas could be reclaimed without upsetting the overall balance of nature in this predominantly swampy landscape. Artificial lakes and beaches were created and, on one tract of reclaimed land, the new Magic Kingdom was constructed.

What fascinates urban planners so much is the fact that this Magic Kingdom was built on a giant concrete pad beneath which, as mentioned earlier, is a whole underground world in which the service systems—from electricity to waste disposal—have been installed, and where the mundane functions of moving personnel and goods can take place. Architects and planners have long advocated the notion of infrastructures, as they are called, as a solution to many of our urban ills. Imagine a city in which all deliveries are made below ground so that the streets are free of trucks! At New York's Rockefeller Center, built in the thirties, and in a few other complexes, limited but successful use had been made of the concept, but it was at Walt Disney World that it received its first large-scale tryout.

Walt Disney World is, of course, free of many of the problems that beset our cities. There are no slums, no school systems, and there is no need to worry about a viable tax base. Thus the Disney organization has not had to deal with certain realities, but this is precisely why they have been able to experiment freely, and the experiments are fascinating and useful.

For all its success as an entertainment center, Walt Disney World is also a valuable laboratory in which systems that may enhance the cities of tomorrow can be tried out. The advanced building code that pertains there has permitted Disney architects and engineers to make use of innovative building techniques. Two of the

FOLLOWING PAGES: An artist's impression of the proposed entrance area for EPCOT (Experimental Prototype Community of Tomorrow). The huge sphere in the center is a geodesic dome which will house the Spaceship Earth theme show.

The medical pavilion at EPCOT will feature a voyage through the human body.

hotels on the property, for example, pioneered a new method of lightweight steel modular construction. Environmental management is taken very seriously. For instance, although an advanced wastewater treatment plant is in operation, further purification of wastewater is achieved by using it to irrigate an experimental tree farm. Energy conservation is exemplified at the Central Energy Plant by using the waste heat from the jet engine exhaust to heat water and operate heat-driven air conditioning systems. An office building has been constructed which is both heated and cooled in a similar fashion using the hot water obtained from a prototype solar collector system, in order to establish the feasibility of displacing conventional heating and cooling systems with large scale solar systems. Experiments are being conducted to establish the feasibility of producing renewable fuels from waste products. A water hyacinth wastewater treatment system will produce a biomass which can be converted to methane by an aerobic digestion process. Eventually, this system may also recycle solid waste along with the hyacinths to produce this synthetic natural gas.

The Magic Kingdom, along with its satellite resort areas, already serves as a living example for town planners. It caters, after all, to more than 13,000,000 people a year and few of them go away dissatisfied. Both above and below ground it has lessons for the future. Aside from its success with transportation systems and services, the intimacy of scale and richness of texture stand as an alternative to the chrome and glass high-rise clusters of our downtown areas. If nothing else, Walt Disney World helps show that there is no one clear-cut solution to the way environments should be created. It shows that the main need is to define the aims of

Plans for the Seven Seas pavilion include an underwater restaurant.

the given environment, then plan accordingly. It is not a question of saying that one thing is right and the other is wrong—it may well be possible and desirable to create pockets of intimacy within high-rise complexes, and architects seem to be moving in that direction—but we should take note of the fact that Walt Disney, unheralded, served to draw attention to possibilities and human needs that were being ignored by orthodox planners.

Walt Disney World is far more than just another theme park—a carbon copy of Disneyland—and the entire area has its futuristic aspects. It is exhilarating, for example, to watch the monorail pull into the cathedral-like lobby of the Contemporary Hotel. The model community of Lake Buena Vista is located here too, but, more importantly, Walt Disney envisioned this huge tract of Florida swampland as the site for his last and possibly most ambitious project, EPCOT. EPCOT stands, quite simply, for Experimental Prototype Community of Tomorrow. When Disney announced his plans for EPCOT, in 1966, he outlined the principles that would govern the project:

> **I don't believe there's a challenge anywhere in the world that's more important to people everywhere than finding solutions to the problems of our cities. But where do we begin . . . how do we start answering this great challenge?**
>
> **Well, we're convinced we must start with the public need. And that need is not just for curing the old ills of old cities . . . EPCOT is . . . an experimental prototype community that will always be in a state of becoming. It will never cease to be a living blueprint of the future . . .**

We don't presume to know all the answers. In fact we're counting on the co-operation of American industry to provide their best thinking during the planning of our experimental prototype community of tomorrow. And most important of all, when EPCOT has become a reality and we find the need for technologies that don't even exist today, it's our hope that EPCOT will stimulate American industry to develop new solutions that will meet the needs of people expressed right here in this experimental community.

What Disney was proposing is reminiscent of some of the visionary schemes dreamed up by architects and city planners in the twenties and thirties—early sketches for EPCOT make this quite clear—but there is one big difference. Walt Disney had proved over and over again that he had the ability to transform his dreams into reality. Unlike earlier visionaries, he had a large and tried organization behind him, and when he spoke he was addressing a ready-made and receptive audience of several million people.

He was not the kind of man to announce a project until he was sure he could follow through on it. Tragically, he was dead just a few months after the plans for his experimental community were unveiled, but the Disney organization has continued to develop the concept and, at the time of writing, there is every reason to believe that EPCOT will be built in the very near future. The team that is planning EPCOT—it includes long-time Disney veterans, ex-astronaut L. Gordon Cooper, Ray Bradbury, and dozens of scientists, researchers, engineers, architects, and others dedicated to the idea of creating a viable tomorrow—is working toward four basic objectives:

ONE: EPCOT will be a "Showcase for prototype concepts," demonstrating practical applications of new ideas and systems from creative centers everywhere.

TWO: EPCOT will provide an "on-going forum of the future,"

192

where the best thinking of industry, government and academia is exchanged to communicate practical solutions to the needs of the world community.

THREE: EPCOT will be a "communicator to the world," utilizing the growing spectrum of information transfer to bring new knowledge to the public.

FOUR: EPCOT will be a permanent "international people-to-people exchange," advancing the cause of world understanding.

In a sense, EPCOT is already underway. Scientists have gathered at Walt Disney World to discuss such subjects as energy conservation and the future of agriculture. Also, many of the systems now in use at Walt Disney World relate directly to the lines along which EPCOT is developing. EPCOT will not, in fact, be so much a separate entity as an integral part of the total Walt Disney World organism, along with the Magic Kingdom and all the resort facilities. Walt Disney did not have a compartmentalized mind. He did not accept the idea that because his primary experience was in the world of entertainment he was prohibited from taking an active interest in practical technology and future planning. His expertise in communications—in the old fashioned art of storytelling—could be applied to science and show business alike. The way that EPCOT and Walt Disney World are developing is a faithful reflection of this.

According to the present master plan, the first phase of EPCOT will consist of two main complexes—Future World and World Showcase—between them occupying an area slightly larger than the Magic Kingdom. Future World will be composed of a number of pavilions devoted to previewing, in dramatic form, alternative technologies available to "the community of the future." The major theme show there, Spaceship Earth, has been conceived as an introduction to the entire concept and meaning of EPCOT. Entering by way of a huge geodesic dome, the visitor will be whisked back through time, watching as layer after layer of culture is stripped away until the journey finally passes the point at which mankind appeared on earth, reaching at last the moment when primitive life first evolved on the planet. Then the unreeling of time will be reversed and the visitor will be carried back toward the present, watching as man, acquiring increasingly sophisticated tools, learns to communicate survival patterns through images and symbols—a voyage that will end up with the contemporary world of computers and data processing and take a glance at the information economy of the future.

Other theme shows will include an energy pavilion, a life and health pavilion, a transportation pavilion, an exploration of the riches of the oceans, and an exhibit devoted to agriculture and the land, emphasizing the theme of living in harmony with nature. In these theme shows, the emphasis will be on finding practical solutions to the problems that confront the modern world. In the energy pavilion, for example, the possibilities of solar power, wind power, new fuels, and a dozen other potential energy sources will be presented in a way that will be meaningful to the layman. The intention is not to say that this or that is the only way of approaching things—there will be nothing didactic about EPCOT—but rather to make people aware of what is available today, and what is likely to be available in the future. Every effort will be made to involve the visitor, to encourage him to participate in the decision-making process, and to allow him to return to his own community with a greater awareness of what he and his representatives can do to encourage the development of new energy sources.

A rather different kind of exhibit in Future World will be the giant Space Vehicle—a mock-up of an extraterrestrial station that will use a 360° movie screen to produce the illusion of voyages to the edge of our galaxy and beyond. Central to Future World will be Communicore—a kind of multileveled plaza of the future—which will link the various pavilions and serve as a focal point where the visitor can experience the communications systems of tomorrow.

At the crossroads between Future World and World Showcase will be an exhibit called the American Adventure inspired by Herman Melville's remarks, "America has been settled by the people of all nations, all nations may claim her for their own . . . We are not a nation so much as a world." Here three spokesmen, Benjamin Franklin, Mark Twain, and Will Rogers—brought to life through the Disney "Audio-Animatronics" process—will conduct visitors through the history of the American people from the first step on Plymouth Rock to the first step onto the moon.

Beyond the American Adventure, grouped around a circular lagoon, will be the pavilions of individual nations from all over the globe. In this World Showcase, cafes, restaurants, and promenades—each built in the architectural idioms of the sponsoring country—will front onto the lagoon, which will itself be used for spectacular water shows. Shopping streets will be found there too, and behind them, in many cases, will be permanent trade exhibits. It is planned that these pavilions will be operated by young adults from each of the nations involved who will live together in a nearby International Village.

This, then, will be the beginnings of EPCOT. At first glance it is all very far removed from the Main Street of Marceline but, as John Hench—one of the men Walt Disney entrusted with the planning and execution of the project—points out, perhaps only a small town boy could be close enough to the basic realities of life to create with a vision of such universal scope.

PART THREE

Fantasy:

the spirit of fantasy in America.) The comedians of the silent screen constantly fell back on the absurdities of antilogic, and exotic fantasies were central to the career and image of many silent stars such as Rudolph Valentino and Douglas Fairbanks. As for the early comic strip, two major figures were Winsor McCay, whose Little Nemo dreamed his way through impossible adventures, and George Herriman who introduced the sublime Krazy Kat strip, a celebration of the irrational, in 1910. (Mickey, when he first appeared, bore a distant family resemblance to Ignatz Mouse, Krazy Kat's tormentor.)

It was only a matter of time before the comic strip and the movies were combined—Winsor McCay himself was a pioneer animator—and fantasy was an almost inevitable outcome of the union. As the first person to grasp and develop the full potential of animation, Disney became, almost automatically, the natural champion of the emerging tradition. Disney did not have Herriman's metaphysical temperament, but Mickey—especially in the first three or four years of his existence—often rose to heights of surrealistic lunacy that were worthy to stand alongside the misadventures of Krazy Kat. This was absurdist fantasy at its best, and it bore little relation to anything anyone had seen on screen before, hence the exhilaration people experienced when they encountered Mickey and his gang for the first time.

At the same time, however, Disney was moving toward the mastery of romantic fantasy, a very different genre but one which, he sensed, could also benefit greatly from the special characteristics of the animated film.

Less than a decade after Mickey was unleashed on the world, Disney gave us *Snow White and the Seven Dwarfs,* the first of his feature-length masterpieces. The subject matter was taken from European folklore, but the film is clearly a landmark in the American tradition of fantasy, a tradition that Disney helped define. It may well be that Disney's chief contribution to America's cultural life is that he was able to unlock doors leading to whole areas of fantasy that had previously been shut off from us. His achievements made many other things possible. Once he had opened the doors, other people were able to pass through and explore areas of fantasy that Disney himself had never dreamed of.

Scenes from *Snow White*.

A drawing for *Toby Tyler Returns,* a 1936 Silly Symphony.

His own fantasy world was rich and varied, however, and we can find it in the parks and in movies as different as the Silly Symphonies and *Mary Poppins.*

Walt Disney was so obviously the dominant figure in his organization that he seldom encountered much passionate opposition to his ideas. One man who was quick to speak his mind, however, was Carl Stalling, the studio's first musical director. (Later, he occupied the same position at the Warner Brothers' cartoon factory, providing scores for Bugs Bunny and Yosemite Sam.) According to Wilfred Jackson, one of Disney's top early animators and directors, Disney and Stalling were constantly battling over the music that Stalling was asked to provide for the Mouse cartoons. The animators continually requested that the music be changed to accommodate the action. Stalling seems to have found this demeaning. Disney, called in to mediate, took the side of the animators, but—after many heated discussions—he promised Stalling that he would, as soon as possible, launch a new series of cartoons in which the animation would be wed to the musical score, rather than vice versa. The result was the Silly Symphonies, which began to appear in 1929.

Toward the end of his life, Stalling claimed that the Symphonies were entirely his idea. The point is academic since he left the Disney organization in 1930, and the Symphonies did not achieve their mature form until two or three years later, though some early examples are not uninteresting.

Skeleton Dance, the first to be produced, was one of the best of these. To music which Stalling adapted from Grieg's "Dance of the Dwarfs," four skeletons emerge from their tombs and perform a dance macabre that was brought to life by the

Walt Disney with models made for *The Three Little Pigs,* 1937.
OPPOSITE: The poster for *Flowers and Trees,* 1932.

animation of Ub Iwerks who, in this instance, displayed his full virtuosity. The Symphonies hit their full stride, however, in 1932 when, starting with *Flowers and Trees,* they began to be produced in Technicolor. Disney was the first producer to make regular use of the new three-strip Technicolor process, which allowed a full chromatic range for the first time, and this caused a considerable stir, giving new impetus to the Silly Symphonies. (The Mickey Mouse cartoons remained in black and white till 1935.) Just a few months after *Flowers and Trees,* the most famous of all the Silly Symphonies—*The Three Little Pigs*—was released and gave Disney his biggest success to date.

Before we discuss that landmark picture, it should be remarked that Disney had displayed considerable foresight in persevering with the Symphony series up to that point. It would have been easier, and perhaps more profitable, to exploit Mickey, but the evidence points to the fact that Walt Disney already had great plans for his organization and wanted to give his artists the kind of broad ex-

Scenes from *Skeleton Dance,* 1929, the first Silly Symphony, and OPPOSITE: Scenes from *Father Noah's Ark,* 1933, and *Midnight in a Toystore,* 1930.

perience that would make them possible to carry out. The Mouse cartoons alone could not have provided that.

The Three Little Pigs not only caused a sensation as a picture but also spawned a hit tune—"Who's Afraid of the Big Bad Wolf?"—which swept the country. The picture was, of course, based on a popular children's story, but at the time, the very worst moment of the Depression, it came to seem a parable about Americans keep-

206

ing the wolf from the door. There is no way of knowing if Disney consciously intended it to be understood that way—he tended to downplay such motives—but the acclaim it received is a good indication of the young Walt Disney's knack of being perfectly in tune with his audience and the times, whether by design or lucky intuition.

Although the Silly Symphonies generally dealt with themes that were overtly

Scene I

First pig building straw house.

Scene II

Second pig building house of sticks

Scene III

Third pig building house of brick

Albert Hurter who contributed much to the look of the Silly Symphonies and the first Disney features.

OPPOSITE: Sketches for *The Three Little Pigs*.

FOLLOWING PAGES: A layout drawing for *Musicland,* 1935

fantastic, they are full of reminders of the American scene as it was in the thirties. The protagonists of *Broken Toys*—one is a doll facsimile of W.C. Fields—inhabit a garbage dump that is itself a catalogue of contemporary household objects. Like any self-respecting hobo, the hero of *The Cookie Carnival* arrives in town riding a box car. In *Who Killed Cock Robin?,* the heroine is called Jenny Wren but bears an unmistakable resemblance to Mae West, and *Mother Goose Goes Hollywood* contains caricatures of several Hollywood personalities. (Katharine Hepburn, for example, appears as Little Bo-Peep.) *Cock of the Walk* offers parodies of Busby Berkeley dance routines, performed by various barnyard creatures, and *Woodland Café* was apparently conceived as a broad parody of café society and the jitterbug craze— with actual bugs aping the dance styles of the day.

At the same time, though, the Symphonies often displayed a kind of rustic quaintness that seems to have been consciously intended to evoke memories of the European fairy-tale tradition. In retrospect, it becomes quite clear how deliberately Disney was leading his artists toward the triumphs of *Snow White and the Seven Dwarfs.*

The look of the Silly Symphonies was greatly influenced by Albert Hurter, a Swiss artist who had trained in European schools before he came to the United States, where he eventually found work in a New York animation studio. Joining the Disney staff in 1932, he displayed a remarkable facility for fantastic, surrealistic invention—a typical sketch shows a human candle shedding wax tears—

THIS PAGE AND OPPOSITE: Layouts for *Musicland*.

FOLLOWING PAGES: A background painting for *Who Killed Cock Robin,* 1935.

Story sketches for Walt Disney's
1939 version of *The Ugly Duckling*.

and for the portrayal of Old World quaintness. Disney quickly recognized that Hurter could be of special value to the studio as an "idea man," so he was relieved of his animation chores and encouraged to spend his working day covering sketch pads with little cameos which were then circulated to the other artists in the hope that they might trigger a fruitful line of thought. Sometimes Hurter's drawings were geared to a specific project that was about to go into production, but often they were unrelated to anything outside of his imagination.

Albert Hurter was, in effect, paid a salary to doodle—but his doodles had a way of finding their way onto the screen. Many of the more bizarre characters who inhabit the Silly Symphonies, and much of the fantastic architecture that helps form their surroundings, originated on Hurter's sketch pad. His imagination had little impact on Mickey and his friends—they still drew their strength from their native American vigor—but it did have a permanent effect on much of Disney's other work. Even the Fantasyland areas of Disneyland and Walt Disney World could probably be traced back to Hurter's drawings.

The Symphonies gave Disney artists an opportunity to prepare for future tasks, and Disney a chance to deal with story material that was not tied to Mickey and the other established characters. With Mickey, Donald, Goofy, or Pluto, once you had come up with a basic situation—a picnic, say—you knew just what was likely to go wrong and how each of them would react to the predictable crisis. After a while, they virtually wrote their own stories and no longer needed Walt's virtuosity. In the Symphonies—although a few characters like the Big Bad Wolf and the Tortoise and the Hare recurred from time to time—each picture was a new adventure.

Chapter Thirteen
SNOW WHITE AND THE SEVEN DWARFS

A study for *Snow White and the Seven Dwarfs*, 1937.

WHEN WALT DISNEY ANNOUNCED THAT HIS ARTISTS were working on a full-length animated feature film, Hollywood was amused. It was conceded that Disney was probably the most successful producer ever of short films, and everybody was ready to grant that Mickey Mouse was a celebrity in his own right, but what audience, it was asked, would sit through an hour and a half of cartoon capers? The pundits were certain that Disney had bitten off more than he could chew. If they had paid more attention to the kind of material that was beginning to find its way into the Silly Symphonies, they might have been a little more cautious in expressing such an opinion.

Disney knew very well that slapstick comedy was only one of the possibilities open to the imaginative animation producer. Even Mickey and the gang relied far more on character and situation than they did on pie-in-the-face routines. As early as 1932, with *Babes in the Woods,* Disney had shown that he could handle a classic

219

OPPOSITE: Snow White at the well.

FOLLOWING PAGES: The dwarfs' cottage. A
background painting for *Snow White*.

children's story without reducing it to parody. (This was one of the first pictures in which Albert Hurter's influence was evident.) The following year, in *Lullaby Land,* the Disney artists animated a child's dream with a subtlety and a sense of fantasy which went beyond anything that is to be found in the early history of animation. In the best Symphonies, a touch of lyricism was almost always a key ingredient.

Disney tended to let ideas coalesce in his head before he ever mentioned them, even to his closest associates, so there's no way of knowing for sure when he first hit on the notion of making *Snow White and the Seven Dwarfs* as an animated feature. Nor is it clear why he picked *Snow White,* though it's known that as a boy in Kansas City he saw a live-action version—it may, in fact, have been the first movie he ever saw. In any case, Disney seems to have gone to some lengths to collect different European versions of the story in book form, and things apparently began to take firm shape in his mind around the spring or summer of 1934. His closest boyhood friend, Walt Pfeiffer, recalls that Disney visited him in Chicago around that time and discussed *Snow White* at length and with great enthusiasm. The first studio memos, outlining the project and inviting suggestions, were circulated in August of that year. As fall approached, new memos were sent out almost daily, either providing information—"Snow White is a Janet Gaynor Type—fourteen years old"—or asking for ideas. (Animators' salaries tended to be low in those Depression years, so the twenty-five-dollar bonuses that were awarded for bits of business that made their way onto the screen were eagerly competed for.) Albert Hurter and other idea men began working on what the key characters might look like—for some time, Snow White was a blond—and a list of possible names, including Cranky, Dirty, Blabby, Awful, Flabby, and Biggo-Ego, was compiled for the dwarfs.

The careful attention Disney gave to the dwarfs, even at the very beginning, is indicative of his understanding of his medium. In literary versions of *Snow White,* prior to Disney, the seven dwarfs had no names. They existed as a group of woodland eccentrics, hardly differentiated from one another and certainly not

221

Studies for *Snow White*.

Adriana Caselotti, the voice of Snow White, and the live model who posed for the woodsman.

plot. (Two entire scenes, representing thousands of man-hours, were cut at the very last minute.) He also worked closely with the music department, making certain that the score would be seamlessly fitted to the action. *Snow White* was probably the first musical in which all of the songs, including such classics as "Whistle While You Work" and "Some Day My Prince Will Come," were planned to arise naturally out of the action and to contribute to our knowledge of the characters or the story line. The first live-action musical to use songs in this way was MGM's *The Wizard of Oz,* which was not released until two years later.

Because of his special kind of operation—other Hollywood studios had to produce forty or fifty pictures a year—Disney was able to give all his attention to this one project and the end result was one of Hollywood's undisputed masterpieces.

In my earlier book, I stated that *Pinocchio* was probably Disney's greatest film, but I have since revised my opinion and now believe that—while *Pinocchio* is still a marvelous achievement—*Snow White* deserves to take top honors. My reason for this change of opinion is quite simple. While researching the first book, I spent many hours in screening rooms viewing all of Disney's animated features and many of the shorts and live-action films. Under those conditions, with no audience to distract me, I was dazzled by the technical brilliance of *Pinocchio,* which has never

229

Early sketches for *Snow White.*

OPPOSITE: A model sheet for the Prince and a page of ideas for the Queen's magic mirror.

Drawing for the bed-building sequence which did not appear in the final version of *Snow White*.

been surpassed, and on the strength of that rated it slightly higher than *Snow White*. Later, however, I had the opportunity to see both pictures again, in a packed theater surrounded by 1,500 other people. The audience loved *Pinocchio* and was as impressed by its brilliance as I had been, but there were moments (very few) when everyone's attention seemed to flag, however briefly. Each scene is magnificent, but occasionally the momentum is lost as the story moves from one scene to the next. When *Snow White* was shown, on the other hand, the audience was enthralled from beginning to end. For the entire running time of eighty-three minutes, everyone was gripped by the story. The audience's concentration was never broken. People shivered as the huntsman stood poised to plunge his knife into Snow White's back; they cheered as the wicked Queen fell to her death. (And this was not an audience of children. It was composed of presumably sophisticated adults at New York's Lincoln Center.)

The reason *Snow White* is a landmark in the history of the movies is, technical considerations aside, that it is a simple story faultlessly told. This may seem like an easy enough thing to achieve but—given the complexity of film making in general

Layout drawing for a scene at the climax of *Snow White and the Seven Dwarfs*.

and animation in particular—it is extremely rare.

Animation does offer the film maker certain advantages. Conventional Hollywood movies rely on the presence of stars, and this can unbalance things. The best screenplay in the world can be overwhelmed by a major star. It is commonly conceded that Greta Garbo was perhaps the greatest female star Hollywood ever produced, yet she never made a picture that came even close to perfection, and this was, perhaps, *because* she was so great a star. When she is on screen, it is difficult to pay attention to anyone else. She dominates every scene, so the ensemble playing is thrown out of kilter. In an animated film such as *Snow White,* on the other hand, the story department and the animators have total control over their characters so that a perfect ensemble can be achieved.

At his very first try, Walt Disney had pulled off what every other important Hollywood film maker dreamed of doing—a full-length film that was precisely tailored to the needs of the American entertainment industry, but which had universal appeal and significance. He had also succeeded in giving definitive American form to an international folk classic.

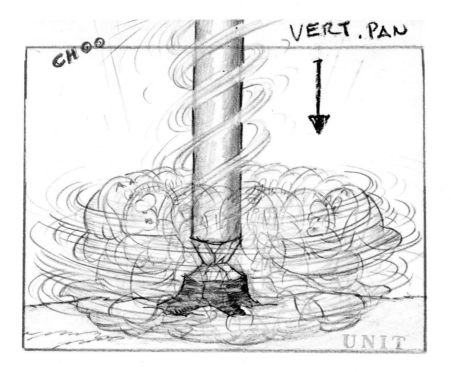

THIS PAGE AND OPPOSITE: Story sketches and layouts for *Snow White and the Seven Dwarfs*.
Often story and layout artists took a scene through dozens of different versions before it
was eventually handed to the animators.

America, a nation of immigrants, has vestiges of many cultures, especially European. These cultures do not become completely American, however, without undergoing some kind of transformation. Millions of American children may have enjoyed *Snow White* before Disney gave us his version, but it was the Disney picture that defined the story for the American public.

There are hard-line critics of Disney who prefer to say Disney destroyed *Snow White,* arguing that he blunted the sublety and charm of the old versions. It seems to me, however, that this totally misses the point. What Disney did, in effect, was to take the essence of *Snow White* and make it the basis of a Hollywood movie. Inevitably things were lost in the process, but much was gained too. Disney was forced to re-invent the story and in doing so he added much that was new and valuable, especially in the way that he developed the characters of the seven dwarfs.

In any case, *Snow White* opened to enthusiastic notices in 1937, and Disney moved on to a new phase of his career. He was now committed to the animated feature and headed a large organization that was rapidly outgrowing his old plant on Hyperion Avenue. The profits from *Snow White* were used to help build a new and much larger studio, which was built on a substantial lot near the Los Angeles River, in Burbank, not far from the giant Warner Brothers lot and Universal City.

The only person who remained sceptical of Walt Disney's success was his father, Elias. When Walt took Elias on a tour of the new studio, the old man asked, "But what can it be used for?"—meaning, "What can it be used for if, as is all too likely, you go bankrupt?" After a moment's hesitation, Walt managed to set his father's mind at rest. "It would make a wonderful hospital," he explained.

Chapter Fourteen
THE GOLDEN AGE OF FEATURE ANIMATION

Geppetto's workshop.

SNOW WHITE AND THE SEVEN DWARFS inaugurated a golden age which was to last barely six years but which saw the production of four more *tours de force—Pinocchio, Fantasia, Dumbo,* and *Bambi.* Each of these was a spectacular achievement, and each was very different from all of the others and from *Snow White.* These pictures, considered alone, could assure Disney a major position in the history of the American film.

Pinocchio was based on Carlo Collodi's Italian classic. Again, however, the spirit and content of the original were greatly altered as Disney refashioned the story for his screen audience. (Some critics have attacked Disney for frightening children with Monstro the Whale and in other sequences of *Pinocchio,* but it should be pointed out that there are other passages in the book, far more scary, which Disney excised.)

After his triumph with his first feature, Disney was anxious to move on to new

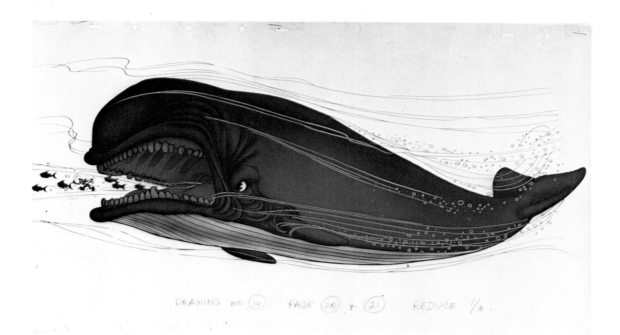

Monstro, the whale.

glories and immediately put the *Pinocchio* project onto a crash schedule. It quickly ran into problems, however—the chief of which centered on the title character himself. Traditional illustrations showed Pinocchio as very much a puppet and so the animators assigned to develop the character—Frank Thomas, Milt Kahl, and Ollie Johnston—began to animate him as a puppet, making him move in a wooden, jerky kind of way. This proved very unsatisfactory, and it was decided that they would have to start over again, giving the character more of the physical attributes of a small boy from the very beginning (except where he is actually suspended from strings). Jiminy Cricket, animated chiefly by Ward Kimball, Woolie Reitherman, and Don Towsley, was also a considerable challenge. As the outlines of the plot began to take shape at story conferences, it became clear that the cricket was becoming far more important to the picture than had originally been anticipated. He was, after all, being asked to serve as Pinocchio's conscience. The difficulty this presented was that a cricket is so small that he tends to get dwarfed by the larger characters. To some extent this could be solved by presenting him in close-up as much as possible, but that was not always a practical solution and so the animators were forced to use all their ingenuity in devising ways to keep him active—making his energy so apparent that it overcame his diminutive size.

Once these initial difficulties had been overcome, however, the project went ahead at full speed. All the experience gained in the first feature gave the Disney

THIS PAGE AND OPPOSITE: Scenes from *Pinocchio*. Made at a time when Disney had finally trained his artists to the level of skill that he demanded, and before the staff was depleted by World War II, this picture represents a technical high point in the art of animation.

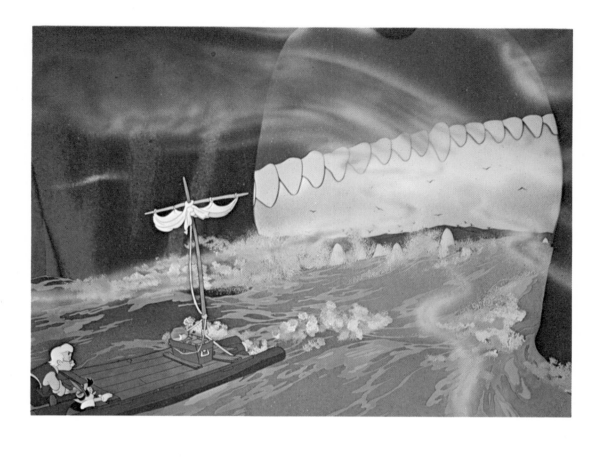

artists tremendous confidence, and they devised scenes of great visual originality. In *Pinocchio,* the camera soars above rooftops and sweeps down on exquisitely rendered panoramas, thus anticipating effects that were not achieved in live-action forms until a couple of decades later when zoom lenses and helicopter shots came into general use. The multiplane camera, employed only sparingly in *Snow White,* came into its own during the production of *Pinocchio,* allowing a great illusion of depth to become a dramatic factor in key scenes and generally enriching the visual texture of the film. The art work itself is stunning. Never before or since have Disney artists produced more spectacular background paintings. Working from studies prepared by Albert Hurter and Gustav Tenggren, a fine illustrator, the background artists conjured up carefully detailed street scenes and interiors. Every brick and cobblestone seems to contribute to the atmosphere of the film. Technically, *Pinocchio* is probably *the* high point of the art of animation up to the present time.

The story of the picture is familiar enough. Geppetto, the old puppet maker, longs for a son and the Blue Fairy grants him his wish by bringing one of his creations, Pinocchio, to life. Pinocchio cannot become a real boy, however, until he learns the difference between right and wrong, and his naivete leads him into all kinds of mischief and trouble and brings him into contact with some of the liveliest and most fully realized villains in the Disney pantheon. The wily fox and his cretinous feline companion are unforgettable as a team of fast-buck artists, and the puppet master Stomboli, animated by Bill Tytla, is probably the most evil character ever to emerge from the Disney studio, a bearded mountain of a man consumed by hatred of the world. Monstro the Whale represents nature at its most terrifying, and the coachman, who tricks "bad boys"—including Pinocchio—into selling their souls, is a model of duplicity. With these, we must include the streetwise hoodlum Lampwick, under whose spell Pinocchio falls—though Lampwick is ultimately a victim rather than a villain.

All these characters do their best to deflect Pinocchio from the straight and nar-

The images on these opposite pages give some idea of the variety of styles that found their way onto story boards. It was left to the layout men and animators to impose a consistant idiom on the movie itself.

FOLLOWING PAGES: Background paintings for *Pinocchio*.

43

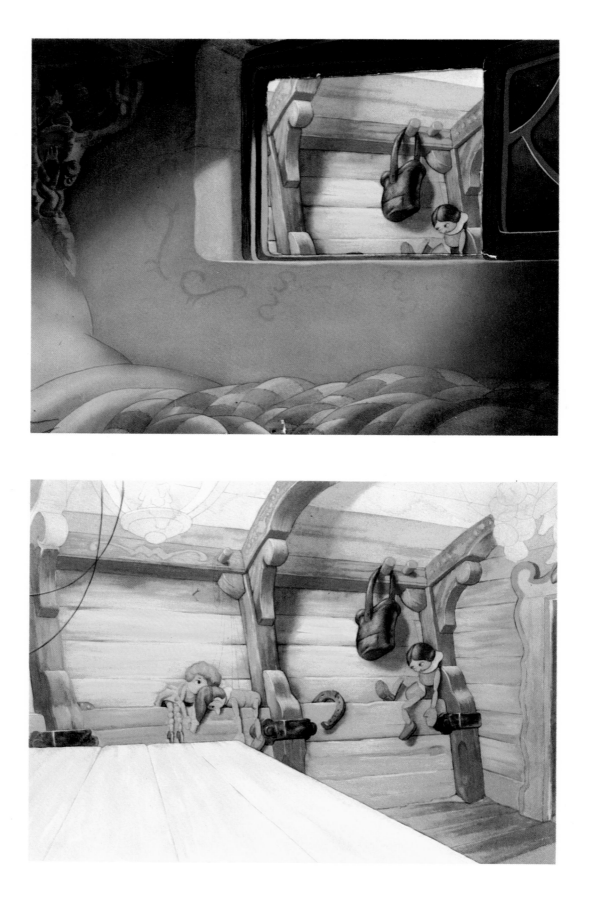

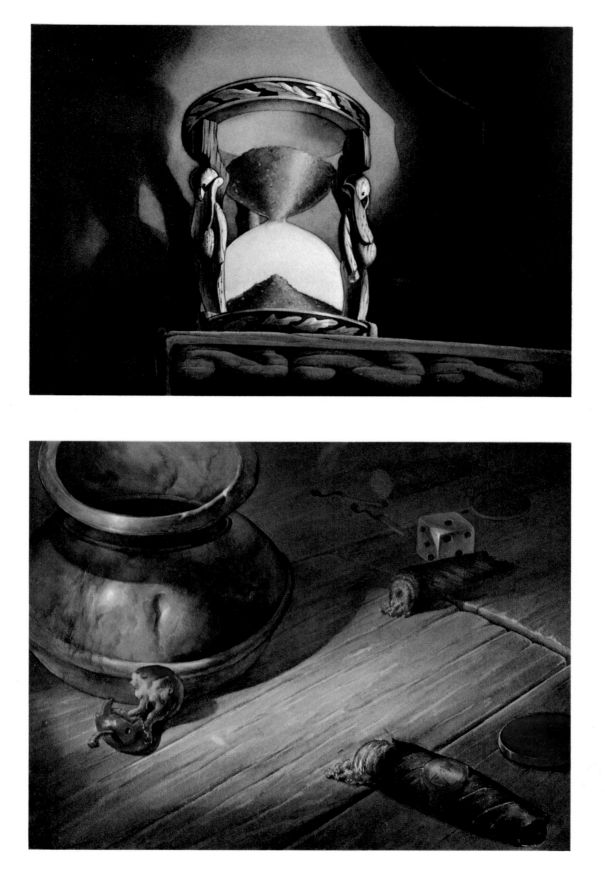

row path, and he, knowing nothing of the ways of the world, is an easy mark. The Blue Fairy gives her godchild a few lessons—as when she causes his nose to grow longer whenever he tells a lie, (by making the wooden nose sprout leaves and even support a bird's nest, the Disney artists greatly enhanced the effectiveness of this scene). Mostly, though, it is left to Jiminy Cricket to protect Pinocchio from himself, a task that he carries out with a unique blend of pomposity and tenacity. (Jiminy's distinctive voice was supplied by Cliff Edwards, also known as "Ukulele Ike," a veteran of vaudeville, radio, and movies.)

In the end—although it does not hold together quite as well as *Snow White*— *Pinocchio* emerged as an exercise in virtuosity, packed with good things. It gives us wonderful characters, plenty of action, good comedy sequences, at least one memorable song ("An Actor's Life for Me"), and Disney artistry at its absolute peak. Certainly it offered the prospective theatergoer his money's worth, but when it was first released it was a box-office failure. Perhaps, though, this is not surprising. War had broken out in Europe just a few months earlier, and it may simply be that people were not in the mood for this kind of entertainment. This may have been aggravated by the fact that the picture evoked an essentially European world—a world that many people wanted to forget about at the time. It is worth noting that an American fantasy, *The Wizard of Oz,* was playing to crowded houses during the first months of the European war.

Pinocchio is, in fact, Disney's most "European" film, but it has many American touches. At least two of the main characters, Jiminy Cricket and Lampwick, are totally American. Lampwick is a first cousin to Leo Gorcey of the East Side Kids, and even Pinocchio is transformed into a kind of American innocent.

If there is one film that matches *Pinocchio* in technical brilliance it is *Fantasia,* and it, too, was a financial failure when it was first released. In this instance, we must observe that Disney was simply ahead of his time, since *Fantasia* has become the most revived and famous of all Disney animated features. Every year it is discovered by a new audience, and it has recouped its initial losses many times over. The reason for this is easy enough to see. *Fantasia* was an extraordinary experiment. People go to see it because there is not anything else remotely like it.

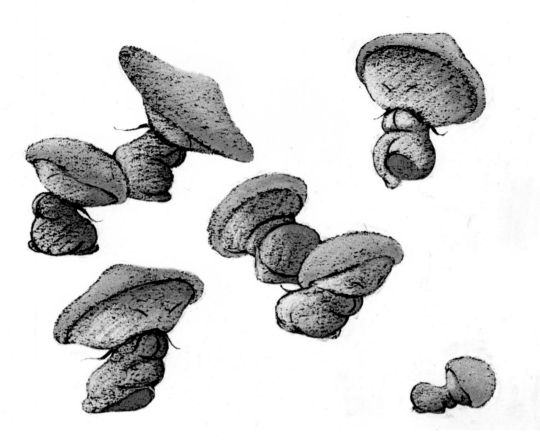

A sketch for the "Nutcracker Suite" segment of *Fantasia.*

As mentioned earlier, it all began with Mickey Mouse. In the late thirties, Walt Disney was worried by Mickey's waning fortunes. (We should remember that at that time the studio was releasing a new short cartoon every three or four weeks.) He hit on the idea of casting Mickey in *The Sorcerer's Apprentice,* using Paul Dukas' orchestral piece of the same name as the musical foundation of the picture. This would have made a picture about fifteen minutes long—a little more than twice the length of the average short—which in itself would have announced the fact that this was intended to be a rather special vehicle. As this idea took shape in Disney's head, he met Leopold Stokowski, maestro of the Philadelphia Orchestra, and the producer asked the conductor if he would be interested in participating in the project. Stokowski was enthusiastic and not only agreed to work on *The Sorcerer's Apprentice* but took the notion several steps further. Why not, he asked, develop a feature film made up of several selections taken from the popular classics? Disney did not have much knowledge of classical music, but he was

A scene from the "Nutcracker Suite."

fascinated by the proposal and immediately set about implementing it.

The project was given a working title—*The Concert Feature*—and preparations were begun. Joe Grant, a specialist in developing character ideas, and Dick Huemer, a veteran animator with a good knowledge of classical music, were put to work listening to literally hundreds of records, looking for pieces that would suit themselves to the medium. Stokowski and Deems Taylor, who was engaged to narrate the movie, added their own suggestions.

Along with *The Sorcerer's Apprentice*, the pieces chosen were Bach's Toccata and Fugue in D minor, excerpts from Tchaikovsky's *Nutcracker Suite*, Stravinsky's *Rite of Spring*, Beethoven's Sixth Symphony (the "Pastoral"), Ponchielli's "Dance of the Hours," from *La Gioconda*, Moussorgsky's *Night on Bald Mountain*, and Schubert's "Ave Maria." The Beethoven selection was a late replacement for Pierné's *Cydalise*—a far lighter piece of music—which had proved intractable to animation because of its too regular rhythmic pattern.

255

THIS PAGE AND OPPOSITE: *Fantasia.* Scenes from "The Sorcerer's Apprentice."

The animation matched with these pieces was as varied as the music itself—ranging from comical whimsy to heavy melodrama—and offered incredible opportunities for artists who, just a few years earlier, had been working in what had to be considered one of the most primitive branches of the entertainment industry. *Fantasia* even features abstraction which, up to that time, had hardly been touched on by other film makers except for a handful of avant-gardists.

It must be said at once, however, that not all segments of *Fantasia* are equally successful. The best, in my opinion, are *The Sorcerer's Apprentice* and "Dance of the Hours," both relatively conventional in idiom (though adventurous within those conventions). *The Sorcerer's Apprentice,* in which Mickey "borrows" the Great Magician's hat and indulges himself in dreams of power which get completely out of hand, is quite wonderful. Disney was absolutely right in thinking that this would make a splendid vehicle for his alter ego. It is the ultimate Mickey Mouse cartoon and, similarly, "Dance of the Hours" can be seen as the last word in Silly Symphonies. In this segment, hippos and elephants pirouette, and ostriches and crocodiles perform *entrechats* in a delicious parody of classical dance. This is the Ballet Russe de Monte Carlo gone mad. Creatures weighing a couple of tons are made to float like Pavlova and leap like Nijinsky. The Disney studio has never produced anything funnier.

There is some choice animation in *The Nutcracker Suite,* especially in the "Chinese Dance" sequence, and the experiments in abstraction, matched to music by Bach, came off remarkably well. *Night on Bald Mountain,* in which the Devil, superbly brought to life by Bill Tytla, summons souls from a sleeping Gothic town, is powerful and features spectacular special-effects animation, but the "Ave Maria" sequence that is tagged on to it is sentimental and unsatisfying. Also disappointing is the "Pastoral" segment in which male and female centaurs—who, by the time they reached the screen, resembled football players and cheerleaders—cavort in an art deco Arcadia strewn with Hellenistic temples and cupolas. The opening, which shows a family of flying horses soaring above the landscape, is splendid, and there

Fantasia. Disney used Stravinsky's "Rite of Spring" to underscore the story of the beginnings of life on earth, a sequence that ends with the Age of the Dinosaurs.

FOLLOWING PAGES: A pastel sketch for the "Pastoral" segment of *Fantasia.*

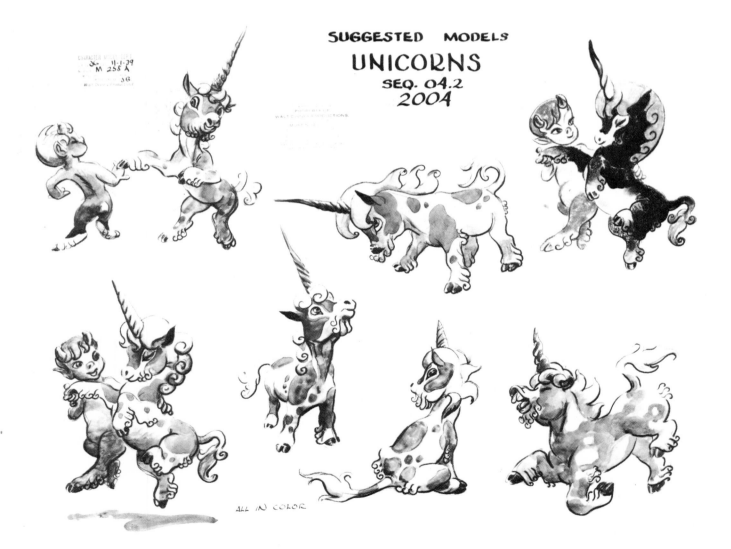

SUGGESTED MODELS
UNICORNS
SEQ. 04.2
2004

ALL IN COLOR

Story sketches for the "Pastoral" segment of *Fantasia*.

OPPOSITE: Early story ideas and a model sheet for the "Pastoral" segment.

FOLLOWING PAGES: *Fantasia*. A water-color study for "Dance of the Hours."

"Dance of the Hours." A cloaked crocodile makes a dramatic entrance.

is some fine comic relief in the form of a drunken Bacchus, but the overall effect is "cute" and hardly fits the splendors of Beethoven's music.

Stravinsky's *Rite of Spring* also proved too much for the Disney artists. Disney himself was unfamiliar with the work when Stokowski proposed it for inclusion in *The Concert Feature,* but Disney was impressed by the powerful rhythms and came up with the idea of using the music to underpin the story of the evolution of life on earth, up till the time of the passing of the dinosaurs. This might have turned out wonderfully, but somehow the studio's efforts missed the mark. The storyboard drawings are powerful enough—some of the undersea sketches are especially fine—but once they had been translated into film they became somewhat turgid and banal.

Fantasia, with good reason, continues to fascinate moviegoers but, in a real sense, it defines some of Walt Disney's limitations. Disney, as he made abundantly clear on many occasions, had no pretensions in the direction of "high art"—to the world of Leopold Stokowski—despite the fact that, throughout the thirties, he had been the darling of the intellectuals, who had recognized his great natural talent. He pro-

266

"Dance of the Hours." Crocodiles conspire around a sleeping hippo.

bably went into the *Fantasia* project thinking of it as a feature-length extension of the Silly Symphonies. What he learned from his encounters with composers like Beethoven and Stravinsky was that "high art" and entertainment do not mix easily. In the wake of *Fantasia,* he seems to have reminded himself that he was, before everything else, an entertainer. A second *Concert Feature,* already in production, was scrapped and the studio staff began to concentrate instead on other projects.

Only sixty-four minutes long, *Dumbo* is one of the shortest of the animated features, and technically it is far more modest than *Pinocchio* or *Fantasia,* but it is one of the most delightful of all Disney films. Faced with the necessity of making up the losses sustained by the two previous features, Disney decided to set his team to work on a project that would utilize their basic skills and their rich experience—their knack with storytelling devices and story development—without bothering too much with the expensive frills. The result was a picture that is charming and relaxed. Disney himself had so much confidence in the story and his staff that he delegated much of the responsibility for the production to some of his trusted veterans. (He was in South America, on his goodwill tour for the State Department,

267

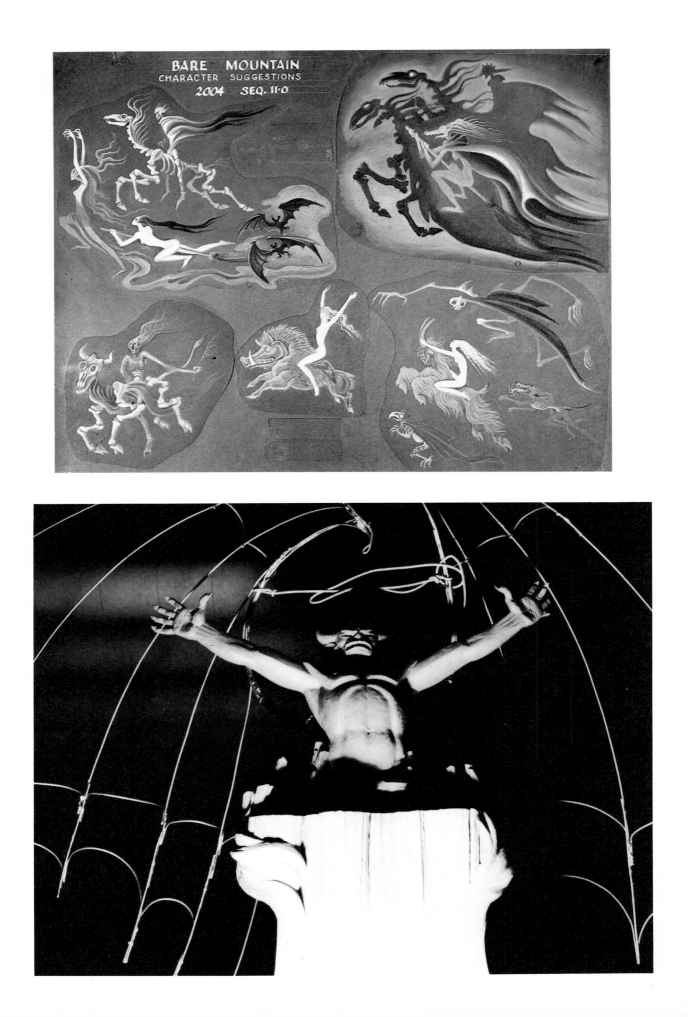

Fantasia: Scenes from "Night on Bare Mountain" and "Ave Maria."

OPPOSITE: A model sheet and a plaster model of Satan for "A Night on Bare Mountain."

during much of this period.) Joe Grant and Dick Huemer adapted the story of the flying elephant for the screen, and the rest of the team set to work with a relish that is evident in the finished product. Bill Tytla and John Lounsbery animated the cruel older elephants, characterized as a group of gossipy matrons, and Norm Ferguson and Karl van Leuven contributed the brilliant "Pink Elephants" episode which takes the form of an hallucination seen by Dumbo's friend, Timothy Mouse, in a moment of drunkenness. Another highlight is provided by Ward Kimball's quartet of zoot-suited crows whose encounter with Dumbo leads him to the discovery that he can fly. Throughout the film, the circus atmosphere is beautifully sustained—interestingly, the clowns are presented as a rather callous bunch—and the music, by Oliver Wallace and Frank Churchill, with song lyrics by Ned Washington, contributes much to the overall effectiveness.

Ward Kimball has said that he knew, from the moment he heard Walt outline the story, that Dumbo had "cartoon heart." This is a crucial point. Not every story, as Disney learned later with *Alice in Wonderland,* lends itself well to animation, but the very thought of a baby elephant sailing above a circus ring on aerodynamic ears is enough to make an animator's mouth water. It is Fantasy at its best.

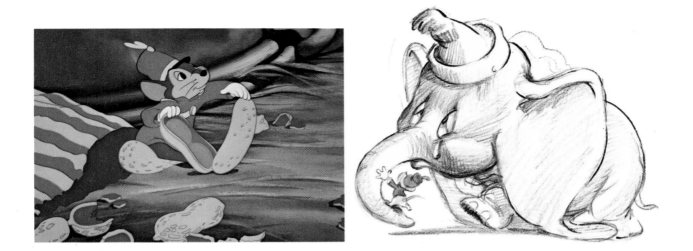

THIS PAGE AND OPPOSITE: Released in 1941, *Dumbo* is one of the most modest yet delightful of all Disney animated features.

FOLLOWING PAGES: The Circus prepares to leave its winter quarters.

Chapter Fifteen
LATER FANTASIES

Tinkerbell, one of the stars of *Peter Pan,* 1953.

BECAUSE OF THE WAR AND OTHER FACTORS, there was a period of several years in which the Disney animation department was forced to subsist with the help of "package" films, pictures like *Make Mine Music* and *Melody Time* which were really assemblages of shorts strung together with a minimum of linking material. Eight years passed between *Bambi* and the release of the next true animated feature, and when the studio began work on this new film it did so with the utmost caution. Many scenes were shot first in live action—just to see if they would work on screen—before the Disney artists embarked on the costly business of animation.

This picture was *Cinderella,* released in 1950, and—though it did not reach the sublime heights of *Snow White*—it was a worthy successor to Disney's first feature, to which it was inevitably compared. Disney involved himself with story development almost as intensely as in the early years. The main story is told in a completely traditional way, with strong comic relief from the ugly sisters and members of

PRECEDING PAGES: *Cinderella.* In her pumpkin coach, heads for the Royal Ball.

OPPOSITE: Cinderella descends the stairs from her garret room.

the royal household, but what makes the picture so successful is the fact that this time-honored tale is counterpointed with the adventures of Cinderella's animal friends—especially Gus and Jacques, two adventurous mice, and Bruno the dog—who are pitted against their own villain, Lucifer, a cat of remarkable rapacity and malignancy.

The result is, again, an Americanization of European folklore. The setting is Ruritanian, but Cinderella is an American princess and the animal characters too seem essentially American (though Gus and Jacques speak pigeon Latin!). The great ball is a fairy-tale version of a senior prom.

Technically, the film is excellent. The character animation is very strong—if there is a weakness it derives from the fact that the Disney artists had become almost too slick at portraying humans by this time—and the atmosphere is well sustained. Once again, Disney obtained a first-rate musical score with songs by Mack David, Jerry Livingston, and Al Hoffman that included "Bibbidi Bobbidi Boo," "So This Is Love," "Cinderella," and "A Dream Is a Wish Your Heart Makes." *Cinderella* was well received by the critics and was a considerable hit with the moviegoing public.

Within the next three years, two more animated features—*Alice in Wonderland* and *Peter Pan*—were released. *Alice* must be counted as a failure. Lewis Carroll's literary brilliance and logical acrobatics did not lend themselves well to the Disney brand of animation. (A few scenes do work well, however, and the film has acquired a cult following.) Disney blamed the failure on Alice herself, saying that she "lacked heart." *Peter Pan,* to which Disney has obtained the rights in 1939, has more to offer and had it been given Disney's full attention it might have been one of the studio's best efforts. As it was, he was very involved with other projects and the characters are not as well developed as they might have been. Tinker Bell, portrayed as a petulant nymphet, is memorable, however, and the film has many good sequences and remains very enjoyable.

During this same period, Disney began to make live-action features in Britain, traveling there every summer to supervise production, and came up with a fine

278

The main subplot of *Cinderella* pits the heroine's animal friends—especially Gus and Jacques, two adventurous mice, and Bruno and the dog—against Lucifer, the evil, feline pet of Cinderella's step mother.

OPPOSITE: *Cinderella* is the archetypal rags-to-riches story.

Disney's version of *Alice in Wonderland,* 1954, has moments of brilliant invention, but the film, taken as a whole, is a disappointment. Disney himself complained that Alice lacked heart.

Sleeping Beauty, 1959.

series of period dramas that includes *Treasure Island, Robin Hood, The Sword and the Rose,* and *Rob Roy, the Highland Rogue. Treasure Island* in particular, starring Robert Newton as Long John Silver and Bobby Driscoll as Jim Hawkins, holds up extremely well. Throughout the fifties and sixties, the Disney studio continued to mine existing veins, producing several live-action pictures every year and turning out a new animated feature at an average of about one every three years.

Sleeping Beauty, which was released in 1959, was one of Disney's few unmitigated disasters. Disney had, it seems, gone to the well once too often so far as the classic fairy tale was concerned. Except for a fine villainess, Maleficent, and her sidekicks—a grotesque army of "Goons"—the characters do not come to life. In *Lady and the Tramp,* Disney artists had made clever use of the wide-screen format, moving their protagonists against broad, realistic panoramas. In *Sleeping Beauty,* by contrast, the wide screen became clogged with overdetailed and highly stylized

FOLLOWING PAGES: *Peter Pan,* 1953, is an enjoyable adaptation of Sir James Barrie's classic.

backgrounds which were quite striking in themselves but tended to get in the way of the action.

101 Dalmatians, which reached the screen two years later, represented a return to the situation-comedy-type plotting of *Lady and the Tramp,* and it is a thoroughly entertaining picture. Again, dogs interact with and mirror human society, and another splendid villainess, Cruella de Vil, is introduced. This was the first feature to make use of Ub Iwerks' process for Xeroxing animation drawings directly onto "cels." This technique saved much labor. Some of the delicacy we associate with the earlier Disney animated films was lost, but, by way of compensation, more of the spontaneity of the animators' drawings was retained.

The Sword in the Stone, a 1963 film adapted from T.H. White's popular book, was moderately successful at the box office but cannot be counted as one of Disney's greatest triumphs. No one who had read the original could fail to notice that the picture totally failed to capture its atmosphere. Where White's text is almost mystical, Disney's film version is, at best, mildly comical.

Happily, the last animated film Walt Disney himself worked on, *The Jungle Book,* was an altogether more characteristic work. Released in 1967, it brought Rudyard Kipling's stories to life—transforming them into contemporary screen fare without damaging their essence. In this picture, especially good use was made of voice talent—one thinks in particular of Phil Harris as Baloo the Bear and George Sanders as Shere Khan, the tiger—and all aspects of the animator's art are integrated into a very satisfying whole.

By far the biggest Disney hit of the sixties, however, was *Mary Poppins.* Starring Julie Andrews and Dick Van Dyke, it combined live action and animation to capture the magic of P.L. Travers' stories. It is a picture that utilized all the expertise of the Disney studio and as such it provided a fitting climax for Walt Disney's film career. It may lack the perfection of *Snow White* and the daring of *Fantasia,* but it certainly demonstrated that Disney still knew how to put together a spectacular production and how to reach out to his audience.

287

Chapter Sixteen
A CHARMED EXISTENCE

Mickey and Pluto.

WHEN WE CONSIDER THE TOTALITY of Walt Disney's career, we cannot help but be impressed by its scope and variety. It is a measure of the magnitude of his success that his television output seems like little more than a footnote to his career taken as a whole, yet the weekly television series has gone through hundreds of episodes over a period of almost a quarter of a century, most of the time remaining high in the ratings. Nor can we overlook *The Mickey Mouse Club,* which ran for more than three hundred episodes, starting in 1955, and created a major teenage star, Annette Funicello.

What Disney did, in effect, was to create his own world, connected to everyday reality yet not really part of it. It was not a private world, though, since anyone who chose to could enter it and, by doing so, could contribute to it. Its continued existence depended not only on Walt Disney's imagination but also on the willing participation of millions of people.

291

Disney's world was distilled from elements he found in the environment he grew up in; it was, for the most part, America purged of problems and heightened by fantasy. It was America transformed by a unique way of seeing and, from the moment of Mickey's debut in *Steamboat Willie,* Disney busied himself with the task of teaching us to see things through his eyes. The extent to which he succeeded can be judged by the facts that the organization he created continues to thrive and that we are still entertained by pictures he made twenty, thirty, and forty years ago. The whole thing was built on a clear idea of his own abilities and responsibilities:

> **The span of years has not much altered my fundamental ideas about mass amusement. Experience has merely perfected the style and the method and the techniques of presentation. My entertainment credo has not changed a whit. Strong combat and soft satire are our story cores. Virtue triumphs over wickedness in our fables. Tyrannical bullies are routed or conquered by our good little people, human or animal. Basic morality is always deeply implicit in our screen legends . . . All are pitched towards the happy and satisfactory ending. There is no cynicism in me and none is allowed in our work.**

One other quotation may be used to state his philosophy even more succinctly. "Laughter," Disney once said, "is America's most important export."

Disney certainly made us laugh, but I believe there is more to it than this. The originality of his viewpoint—it was apparent from the first Mickey Mouse cartoons—liberated laughter, and our sense of fantasy, from stifling conventions. Think, for a moment, of the way Disney's animated creatures move. They have a comical grace which, when these films were first shown, had never been seen before. Hippos and elephants are released from their compact with the laws of gravity and float like feathers. Goofy falls from the top of a skyscraper and en-

Walt Disney with his most famous creation, 1931.

counters a convenient flagpole which catapults him back to the safety of a ledge.

Animated characters lead a charmed existence because they are not bound by the laws of nature. They obey those laws so long as it is useful to do so—that gives them a footing in our world—but, whenever necessary, they can stretch them, bend them, and even reverse them by the exercise of sheer willpower. Whatever catastrophes befall them, they are never in real danger because they are blessed by the freedom that we all experience in dreams. For them, anything is possible; and we are not merely told that this is so, we can see it with our own eyes.

Animators before Disney knew that all this was possible, but it was Disney, with his great sense of structure, who was the first to make it work coherently and who had the courage to invent bigger and more spectacular dreams.

It was this that made him a great American original: a liberator of the imagination.

CHRONOLOGY

1901: Walter Elias Disney is born, December 5, in Chicago, Illinois. His father, Elias, is the proprietor of a small construction company. His mother, the former Flora Call, is an ex-school teacher. Walt is the youngest of four boys. A sister, Ruth, will be born three years later.

1906: Elias moves his family to a 48-acre farm near the small town of Marceline, Missouri.

1910: Elias sells the farm and the family moves again, this time to Kansas City, where Elias invests in a newspaper delivery service. Walt and his brother Roy find themselves rising at 3:30 in the morning to meet the trucks of the Kansas City Star.

c1915: Walt attends Saturday morning art classes at the Kansas City Art Institute. At about this same time he begins to sneak out in the evenings so that he and his friend Walt Pfeiffer can take part in amateur talent contests. (Elias disapproves of show business.) On these occasions, Walt Disney often impersonates Charlie Chaplin.

1917: Walt's parents return to Chicago where Elias becomes a partner in a small manufacturing business. After spending part of the summer as a news butcher on the Sante Fe Railroad, Walt rejoins the family. He attends McKinley High School—contributing drawings to the school paper—and obtains further art instruction from a newspaper cartoonist called Leroy Gossett. A few months after his return to Chicago, Walt, although under age, manages to enlist in the Ambulance Corps.

1918: Walt arrives in France shortly after the armistice and serves there for several months.

1919: Returning to the USA, Walt heads for Kansas City and finds work in a commercial art studio where he meets another young artist, Ub Iwerks. The two become friends and set up their own business, then move on to the Kansas City Film Ad Company which produces crude animated pictures.

1920: In his spare time, Walt produces his own first cartoon, a reel of topical gags for the Newman Theater in Kansas City. Following this, he manages to raise enough money to launch the Laugh-o-Gram Company where he is joined by Iwerks and several other local artists including Rudolph Ising, Hugh and Walker Harman, Carmen "Max" Maxwell, and Red Lyon. During the next couple of years they take on any kind of film-making job that will keep the business afloat, but manage to produce a series of animated fairy stories including *Cinderella, The Four Musicians of Bremen, Goldie Locks and the Three Bears, Jack and the Beanstalk, Little Red Riding Hood* and *Puss in Boots*. These one-reelers combine traditional subject matter with contemporary gags.

1922: Walt begins work on *Alice's Wonderland* in which a real girl, shot in live action, finds herself involved in the adventures of a group of cartoon characters. This project exhausts the company's resources and Disney is forced to close the studio.

1923: Walt moves to California to join his brother Roy who is recovering from a bout with tuberculosis in a US Navy sanitarium in the Los Angeles area. Walt searches, without luck, for work in the Hollywood Studios. He has brought *Alice's Wonderland* with him and this is seen by a distributor who offers him a contract to produce a series—the Alice Comedies—based on this picture. Roy becomes Walt's partner, handling the business side of the operation, and they rent a storefront studio in the Silver Lake section of Los Angeles. Soon they are joined there by Iwerks and other members of the old Kansas City team.

The Alice Comedies are a modest success and almost sixty are produced in a period of less than four years.

1925: Walt marries Lillian Bounds, a secretary at the studio.

1927: Alice is phased out and replaced by a new all-cartoon series based on the character of Oswald the Lucky Rabbit. Towards the end of the year, the success of the Warner Brothers sound picture, *The Jazz Singer,* throws the motion picture industry into a panic.

1928: Because of a contractual oversight, Walt loses the Oswald character to his distributor, who also hires away some of Disney's top assistants. Forced to find a replacement character, in a hurry, Walt comes up with Mickey Mouse. Ub Iwerks designs Mickey and they immediately begin work on the first Mouse cartoon, *Plane Crazy.* Before this is released, however, Walt decides they must take advantage of the "talkies" craze which is sweeping the country. Work begins on a second Mouse cartoon, *Steamboat Willie,* which is planned from the outset as a sound picture. Walt takes it to New York where music and effects are added. *Steamboat Willie* becomes the first sound cartoon. It opens at the Colony Theater in Manhattan on November 18, 1928, and receives enthusiastic notices. Audiences are enchanted and within a matter of months Mickey Mouse has become a household name.

1929: Walt Disney launches a new cartoon series, the Silly Symphonies.

1930: Ub Iwerks leaves the Disney organization to found his own studio. Despite this loss—Iwerks is the greatest animator of the day—both the Mouse cartoons and the Silly Symphonies go from strength to strength, thanks largely to Disney's brilliance as a story editor. Mickey Mouse Clubs begin to spring up in movie theaters throughout the United States.

Pluto—though he has not yet been named—makes his first appearance in *The Chain Gang.*

1932: A Silly Symphony, *Flowers and Trees,* is the first movie to be made in three strip Technicolor. A few months later, *The Three Little Pigs* provides Disney with his greatest success to date.

Goofy, to be known for a while as Dippy Dawg, makes his debut in *Mickey's Revue.*

1934: Preliminary work begins on *Snow White and the Seven Dwarfs,* the first Disney feature-length project. Donald Duck debuts in *The Wise Little Hen* and quickly establishes himself as a popular favorite.

1935: This might be considered the peak year for short cartoons from the Disney studio. All the top animators are still working on shorts. (Soon they will transfer to features.) Mickey Mouse cartoons go into full color and almost every picture that comes out of the Disney plant this year—*The Tortoise and the Hare, Music Land, The Band Concert, Cookie Carnival, Broken Toys, Cock of the Walk, Mickey's Garden,* etc.—is a small masterpiece.

1936: Work on *Snow White* shifts into high gear.

1937: *Snow White* is released to enthusiastic reviews and public adulation.

1939: The Disney organization begins its move from the old Hyperion Avenue studio to its new headquarters in Burbank.

1940: *Pinocchio* and *Fantasia* are released. Although these are Disney's most spectacular films, from a technical viewpoint, both are box office failures when they first appear.

1941: *Dumbo* reaches the screen and begins to recoup the losses sustained by the two previous features. Another 1941 release, *The Reluctant Dragon,* starring Robert Benchley, is the first Disney picture since the Alice Comedies to make extensive use of live action footage.

1942: *Bambi* is launched to an enthusiastic reception.

1943-45: The Disney studio makes many training films for the federal government and the armed services, pioneering techniques in "limited animation." *Victory Through Air Power,* a movie about strategic bombing theories of Major Alexander de Seversky, is produced. Cartoons like *Der Fuehrer's Face* and *Educa-*

tion for Death satirize the Nazis, while *Saludos Amigos* and *Three Caballeros* look to the South American market.

1946: *Make Mine Music*
       Song of the South

1947: *Fun and Fancy Free*

1948: Melody Time
       So Dear to My Heart

1949: For economic reasons, Disney has been forced, since *Bambi,* to concentrate on films that either grouped together a number of shorts *(Make Mine Music)* or combined live action with animation *(Song of the South).* Now he begins to move back towards his old standards with *Ichabod and Mr. Toad,* a release that combines two longish animated stories. This year also sees the production of *Seal Island,* the first of the True Life Adventures, and the launching of Buena Vista, Disney's own distribution company.

1950: *Cinderella,* the first true animated feature since 1942, is released and is welcomed by critics and public alike. Disney also moves into the field of all live-action film with *Treasure Island,* made in England.

1951: *Alice in Wonderland*

1952: *Robin Hood* (live action version).
       During this year two companies—WED and Disneyland, Inc.—are set up to plan and finance Disney's first theme park.

1954: *Peter Pan*
       The Sword and the Rose
       The Living Desert
       Rob Roy, Highland Rogue
       The Vanishing Prairie
       20,000 Leagues Under the Sea

In October, the Disneyland television series debuts on ABC.

1955: *Davy Crockett*

Lady and the Tramp
The African Lion
The Littlest Outlaw

Disneyland opens to the public and the Mickey Mouse Club is launched on television.

1956: *The Great Locomotive Chase*
Davy Crockett and the River Pirates
Westward Ho the Wagons

1957: *Johnny Tremaine*
Old Yeller

1958: *The Light in the Forest*
Tonka

1959: *Sleeping Beauty*
The Shaggy Dog
Darby O'Gill and the Little People

1960: *Toby Tyler, or Ten Weeks With a Circus*
Kidnapped
Pollyanana
Ten Who Dared
The Swiss Family Robinson
The Sign of Zorro

1961: *101 Dalmatians*
The Absent Minded Professor
The Parent Trap
Nikki, Wild Dog of the North
Greyfriars Bobby
Babes in Toyland

1962: *Big Red*
The Legend of Lobo

In Search of the Castaways

1963: *Son of Flubber*
   Miracle of the White Stallions
   The Incredible Journey
   The Sword in the Stone

1964: *The Misadventures of Merlin Jones*
   The Moon-Spinners

The most important release of the year is *Mary Poppins,* one of the biggest box-office hits of all times and the recipient of thirteen Academy Award nominations and five Oscars. Among the Oscars, one is awarded to Julie Andrews as Best Actress and another goes to Disney's old Kansas City partner, Ub Iwerks, for Special Visual Effects. (Iwerks had returned to the Disney studio in 1939.)

1965: *Those Calloways*
   That Darn Cat

1966: On December 15, Walt Disney dies of lung cancer. He has been working on *Jungle Book*, the last animated feature of his career, and plans for Walt Disney World. Shortly before his death, he unveils the Walt Disney World project to the public, placing an especial emphasis on EPCOT (Experimental Prototype Community of Tomorrow).

1971: Walt Disney World opens to the public.